The
Polish
Prince

THE
POLISH
PRINCE

BY BOBBY VINTON

M. Evans & Company / New York

Thanks are due to the Chappell Music Company for permission to reprint lyrics from "Playmates" by Saxie Dowell. Copyright © 1939 by Anne-Rachel Music Corporation. Copyright renewed, controlled by Chappell & Co., Inc. International copyright secured. All rights reserved. Used by permission.

Thanks also to Pedro Music Corp., Galahad Music, and Morning Music Ltd. for permission to reprint lyrics from "My Melody of Love." Original music: Henry Mayer. English lyrics: Bobby Vinton. Published in the U.S. by Pedro Music Corp. and Galahad Music. Published in Canada by Morning Music Ltd., Mississauga, Ontario. Copyright 1974 Pedro Music Corp.

Library of Congress Cataloging in Publication Data

Vinton, Bobby.
   The Polish prince.

   1. Vinton, Bobby.   2. Singers—United States—
Biography.
   II. Title.
ML420.V384A3   784'.092'4 [B]   78-15059
ISBN 0-87131-270-0

M. Evans and Company, Inc.
216 East 49 Street
New York, New York 10017

Design by Ginger Giles

Manufactured in the United States of America

9 8 7 6 5 4 3 2 1

ONE
Everything's Coming Up Polish

The warm Chicago evening was crackling with excitement. All of us had come here, to a fine old auditorium, the Stadium, with the feeling that something special was going to happen. The electricity of a celebration was in the air: children in brightly colored costumes were dancing to polkas in the lobby, and the banners of various Polish organizations festooned the hall. They were here in strength, and proud of it: the American Congress, the National Alliance, the Roman Catholic Union, the Women's Alliance of America. The names of Copernicus and Kosciusko were lovingly embroidered on dresses and jackets; here and there women wore roses in their hair and men sported caps lavishly decorated with the emblem of a red eagle. The word was going around that an Irish mayor had declined dinner with a Norwegian king to come to sing with a Polish prince.

There were two loud knocks on my door, and my pulse began racing. I knew what the next words would be: "Fifteen minutes, Mr. Vinton!" I turned to my buddy, Ed Schwartz, with the question that's always in the back of an entertainer's mind. "How many people are out there?"

He laughed. "Maybe five thousand—so far. This is one night you won't have to worry about filling the place." Ed has a finger on the pulse of Chicago, as one of its most popular disc jockeys on the clear-channel station WIND. You could be driving just about anywhere in the Midwest, in the middle of the night, and count on tuning in to Ed's soothing voice. And when everybody else was afraid to play my Polish melody, he gave it a spin. And here we were. "But you're going to split that suit right up the middle," he added.

"Too tight?" Frank Ortiz had made two costumes for me because there wasn't time for a fitting. He had flown them up from Galveston this afternoon. And there on the wall in front of me was hanging the larger of the two jackets, with a red eagle triumphantly emblazoned across the back. Funny, I thought, how a tailor who was born in Mexico would know how to put the Polish eagle and the Polish colors on just right. The zipper stuck, and as I fumbled nervously with it the door flew open and my right-hand man, Vince Carbone, shouted the good news. "There must be ten thousand out there and they're still coming in!"

"That's still only half full," I answered. "Now, who knows how to unjam a zipper?" And another funny thought crossed my mind. This was my Polish night; these were my people. But do people really know that Vinton is my real name and it's as Polish as kielbasa? Here were Schwartz, and Carbone, and Daley. . . . Was the mayor really coming? As if to answer my unspoken question, the best-known Polish man in Chicago walked in the door. I could hear the polka music from the lobby over his voice.

"Fifteen thousand, I'd guess," said Roman Pucinski. "Bobby, you're going to fill the place. And the mayor's on his way for that last seat." That was good enough for me. The alderman, Daley's right-hand man, had taken me under his wing from the moment of our first meeting, when we taught the Irishman to sing *"Moja droga, ja cie kocham. . . ."* Now there were only three minutes to show time, and I was still not dressed. I tried to remember which way to go on stage. Roman's face lit up.

"Listen to that!" he said, as a wave of applause swept over the auditorium. "Daley just came in— they're introducing him." I stepped into the hallway in time to hear the orchestra striking up "My Melody of Love." I was on. Before I knew it I was walking onstage, into the glare of the spotlights, and twenty thousand people rose as one to thunder their approval. Over the roar of the crowd came the words that sent shock waves through my body: "Ladies and gentlemen, the Polish Prince!"

In that moment, for the first time in my life, I felt there was meaning in my work. Everything had been building up to this. This was why I had struggled so hard—not to give just a song, but to give something of

7

myself, and to achieve something for other people with what I had inside me. It had always been there, only I didn't know it. That same Polish eagle that was on the back of my jacket in this moment of triumph had flown over the bandstand in the Polish Falcons Hall in Canonsburg where I had played my first public performance, as a teen-ager more than twenty years before.

As I looked out at all those beaming faces, at all those gloriously costumed children, at a proud mayor, I felt it was true: I was a prince. I *had* done something special, the way a leader in those romantic days of the Middle Ages had done, a prince fighting for his people. And I knew then, too, that the Polish people had done something for me: they had given me a new life and a new reason for singing. Only two years before, I had performed in this same city in front of an audience of—twelve people.

As the applause died down and a hush settled over the auditorium, I felt a surge of power building between us. "I want to make an announcement," I said. "Whatever is going on here this evening, I call it—Polish power!" And on that October evening in 1975, our hearts danced and sang with a spirit of ethnic pride that would spread beyond an entertainment hall, beyond Chicago, beyond culture or race or religion.

In a sense I've never had a comeback: I've always grown in my profession a little bit each year. But if you look only at one side of me—as a recording star or an entertainer or an actor—my life might seem to be a series of ups and downs. I have made movies, but I haven't proved myself as an actor. I've had my own television show, and then dropped it. I've set records for attendance at some of the most prestigious clubs in the country. In the record industry, I have a distinction most people don't realize: between 1962 and 1972, according to *Billboard* magazine, I had more number one hits than any other male singer. And when you sell more than 30 million records, as I have, you know you're among the leaders in your field. . . .

Perhaps there's nowhere to go but down after this kind of success. In any case, even though my earnings had steadily increased from all sources, by 1972 I knew I had reached a kind of plateau. I wanted to go on to something new in the recording business, but I wasn't the bright young face, anymore, that record companies were always looking for. Could I keep on selling records by changing myself to fit the times, to appeal to a younger market of record-buyers?

My first and only record company up to that time didn't think so. In 1972 Epic decided to drop me, by the simple expedient of not renewing my contract. It's no different in the record business than in the insurance business or the Hula-Hoop business: everybody wants to stay current. In our youth-dominated culture, the desire to keep up to date often results in a lopsided catering to the young. And in the record industry, especially, the young account for a very high percentage of pop record sales. Epic Records knew I had sold 30 million records for them—but there *couldn't* be another 30 million in me, so they would find somebody who had that potential. I had been with them for almost fifteen years.

I told my friends at the agency that represented me—Lee Salomon, Sid Epstein, Artie Moskowitz, Lee Stevens, Dick Fox, Dick Allen, and others at William Morris—that I was without a recording contract for the first time in my professional career, but I wasn't worried. I was soon to discover, however, that their work for me was going to get harder. You can have all the confidence in the world, but you also need the confidence of talent buyers and show promoters and impresarios if you want to keep getting good bookings.

The repercussions of being dropped by my record company spread throughout the business. I had been winning a following in the biggest entertainment market of all—Las Vegas. I started there by filling in for other acts when a headliner was ill, or as an opening act for such stars as Don Rickles, Jerry Lewis, Sheckie Green, and Phyllis Diller. From second billing I then moved up to my own act in one of the lounges of the Hilton, and that's perhaps the toughest act of all. Because the audience *knows* you're not a headliner in one of the main rooms, you have to overcome the noise and the distractions and the attitude of the crowd that comes across as "Prove yourself, buddy." (Incidentally, look in the lounges for the talent of the future—there are so many unrecognized performers there waiting for a break.) That's where I was waiting, and a friend named Bill Miller, a big talent buyer, kept saying, "One of these days I'm going to do something for you," and before long he did. A headliner at the Flamingo, which was owned by the Hilton, had to drop out in the middle of his

10

contract, and Miller recommended me for the spot. So all of a sudden the audience looked up and saw *me*, when the night, before, the billboard had said some-one else. I quickly learned it was easier to come across to a main-room audience than a lounge audience; one day I did three lounge acts and two main-room shows, just about walking off one stage and onto another, and I was appreciated far more on the main stage. Maybe that's why, in spite of my success at the Flamingo, I wasn't picked up by the hotel for the following season. They had heard I was being dropped by Epic and that was like dropping back to being a lounge act.

In the follow-the-leader system of running an in-dustry, as well as picking your entertainment, every-body is impressed by billboards. Everybody thinks the other guy knows what he's doing. If you're going down, nobody wants to second-guess the trend. Even your friends don't come around. So there I was, can-celed by my record company and whistling Dixie in Vegas. Back home in California, I twiddled my thumbs for a while and settled into my stock-in-trade: touring. I could always play on the road—at county fairs and little clubs—and I always will. But I wasn't convinced I had achieved anything near my potential in life. And I wasn't discouraged; I have always had the feeling that something big was going to happen and change things completely for me. From the first time I had seen movies about the lives of Benny Goodman or Glenn Miller or Al Jolson I was inspired. I had learned from these stories that nothing really good in life came easy; in fact, the harder the work the bigger the reward. It was a simple philosophy, but I

11

will never knock the power of films, because I know they influenced and motivated me. I came to believe that the finest compliment the world could give a person was to make a movie of his life. Way in the back of my mind was the hope that someday, somehow, I would be up on that silver screen, and I even told myself to do some interesting things to make the movie a good story!

At least one interesting thing was about to happen.

I checked with my agency, William Morris, the way a lovelorn soul checks the mailbox. What was going on in Las Vegas? Were there any movie parts coming up? Were any of the other record companies interested in picking me up? I had experimented with several ideas for records, to try to catch on again in the pop music field. At the agency there were specialists for each type of booking: Freddie Moch was in charge of Las Vegas for me, and Tom Illius handled Reno–Lake Tahoe. Both said nothing was happening. Not even at the Flamingo? I queried. Forget it, Freddie said; Las Vegas is booked for the year.

Now, I have always trusted my agents' judgment—in fact, William Morris people have worked so hard for me and we're on such good terms that I don't need a go-between, a manager, to facilitate our relationship. But I also like to know firsthand what's happening with my audience. So I asked my wife, Dolly, to start packing for a short vacation. We had just had our fifth child, and it was time for something special. Since I'm away from home much of the time in my work, we usually don't like to travel when we don't *have* to. When the kids are out of school, we can sometimes all go to a performance date together. This was different.

"Just the two of us?" Dolly asked, with that honeymoon twinkle in her eye.

"Why not? Let's get away and do some thinking."

"Hawaii? Mexico?"

"No, not that far," I said. "Let's go to Vegas. Something's going to happen."

Dolly has learned to put up with my hunches. She knows I've always had to make my own breaks. And she has also survived that difficult situation—a show-business marriage—just because I am away so much of the time. When I do come home, she says, it's another honeymoon each time. We're forced, too, to be stronger as parents, as well as wife and husband, because of all the travel in my business. This time, at any rate, Dolly was well aware that Las Vegas was preying on my mind. She knew I had to go there and find out why all those other guys were on the billboards, and not me. What were they doing that pulled the customers in, that I couldn't do? What would I have to do to make my act stand out?

As at other critical times in my life, I looked back then into my past as a guide to the right course of action. When I was trying to break into the business in Pittsburgh as a teen-ager, I instinctively went where the action was. I used to take the bus to New York and hang around the recording studios. I knew something would happen that couldn't happen over a telephone or in an envelope. I learned from my father, at the tender age of fourteen, that you had to go where they

13

were hiring and not wait for the performances to come to you. His orchestra was my roots, as much as my Polish neighborhood. But I didn't analyze it—I just acted on it.

Our first evening in Las Vegas started out quiet enough. We took in a couple of shows, and I wasn't enough of a celebrity to get an especially good table. The next afternoon, Dolly rested and I decided to scout around. As I was walking through the casino, a stranger walked right up to me with a big grin on his face. "Say, you're Bobby Vinton, aren't you?" the man in the pin-striped suit asked excitedly.

Even in celebrity-wild places like Las Vegas, I'm not the kind of guy who's easily spotted as a star. If they put my picture on the cover of *Time* magazine, I wouldn't stand out at a newsstand. But this gentleman knew me and seemed impressed. So I did a double-take and tried to remember if this was an old classmate, or a disc jockey, or one of my wife's relatives. As if to explain, he said, "'Blue Velvet' is my wife's favorite record." And then he identified himself as Dan Wolford, the new manager of the Flamingo. In fact, he had been on the job for only a day or so. I was delighted to happen onto him, especially when he said, "How come you never work Las Vegas anymore?"

I thought to myself: I'd give my right arm to get back here. So I answered quickly, "Nobody asked me."

"Then let me ask you," he said, and ten minutes later we were discussing a headline act and a contract and—money. Dan Wolford knew what I had made

14

when I was working the lounge here. I knew that *he* knew. But for the first time in a long time I began to think positively about myself. I had always dwelled on my weaknesses as a performer. And I think I had been too honest, even naïve, when it came to dealing with talent buyers. Instead of selling myself short this time, I took a gamble on myself—what better place than Las Vegas?

He thought over my price. "But that's twice what you made last time, Bobby."

"Sure," I said, "but if you expect me to draw like the other headliners around here, you're really getting me for half price." What I said was true. No matter what I made before, if I performed up to expectations I was still working at half the going rate. Again, I was thinking back to my father's bandleader days, when he told me to go all out, to give 100 percent, or nothing. And Wolford was not the type to hedge, either. He could have dropped the whole matter then and there, but he wouldn't bargain. A big-name entertainer like Sinatra or Dean Martin can draw crowds just by putting his name on the billboard, but I certainly hadn't reached that stage. And in Las Vegas a performer has to draw consistently or he's soon replaced. What it all came down to was whether Wolford really believed I could do it. And as a new manager—he wasn't even the talent buyer—he sensed he had an opportunity right now to make himself a hero by "discovering" someone everyone else had overlooked. He said that when I opened at the Flamingo it would be a great engagement. I think he had more faith in the business I would do than I had.

As the adrenaline was pumping through my body he suddenly looked up, smiled, and extended his hand. "You're a good businessman, Bobby. Welcome back to the Flamingo!"

I danced up to the room to tell Dolly how I had made my biggest crap shoot in Las Vegas—but not at the tables. And then I telephoned Freddie Moch at the agency. "I thought you said Vegas was booked solid," I said with glee. "Well, I'm calling from the Flamingo and I just shook on a deal."

"Impossible." Who'd you talk to?"

"Dan Wolford, the new manager."

"Oh, that guy. He's just temporary."

"I don't care if he's just passing through. I've got a headline spot and the price is right." Dan Wolford was as good as his handshake, and the contracts went through in a few weeks. And now I had to put together an act to merit the confidence he had shown in me.

It's customary in the business to break in your act at another location before doing a headline show in the "entertainment capital of the world." And so I had lined up a performance at another Hilton hotel, the Shamrock in Houston. It was timed to celebrate one of those Super Bowl play-off games, and for me it had an additional interest. Another boyhood dream of mine was to be a football player, before I had ever imagined myself as a bandleader or singer. And here in Houston, after all these years, I had my first chance to meet some famous players up close. Most impressive to me was the friendliness of people like Hank Stram, then coach of the Kansas City Chiefs and today one of my close friends, and the family of Vince Lombardi, who

16

had coached the Green Bay Packers to many championships before his untimely death. I began to notice that Polish people like Hank were becoming more and more important in my life.

With good feelings all around, it turned out to be a rousing show that evening, and Baron Hilton led the applause. He came backstage and surprised me by saying he owed me an apology. "Three standing ovations isn't bad," he began. Then he told me that he was originally against Dan Wolford's hiring me at the Flamingo. "I thought he had made a mistake. But I can see you're a great entertainer and I'm delighted you're with my organization."

"I'm glad to hear that," I said. "Why don't you tell Dan yourself?"

"You're right. I was a little hard on him."

It was now the early hours of the morning in Houston but I said, "Let's call Dan in Vegas and talk to him."

He got a sleepy Dan Wolford on the phone.

"About this Vinton," he said gruffly. "I saw him perform tonight." There was a moment's silence on both ends of the line. Then Hilton laughed. "He's the greatest. You made the right move and I was wrong. I apologize, Dan!"

As I looked back on that crucial meeting in the casino with Wolford, I was almost frightened by the absolute confidence he had in me. "You're going to do well," he kept saying. When we discussed the type of show I would put on, I suggested some sort of novelty, a gimmick to add to my ordinary performance. I wanted to wake these people up! "Relax," he said,

17

"and just keep doing what you've done all along. You don't need any tricks." The word was going around that he had such blind faith in me he must not know anything about talent! And he kept telling everyone that I was going to be a big surprise.

Behind every surprise is a lot of patient home-work—and Wolford had done his. He talked me up with all the help. The little guys were pulling for me. The switchboard operators were told to answer the phone, "Flamingo, where Bobby Vinton is now appearing nightly!" Over the years I had spent a lot of time talking with people in the coffee shops to find out how the big tours select their shows; I was friendly with the tour promoters, the bus drivers, the secretaries. Some of these are "deals" with reduced ticket prices, but they can put three hundred people in a room at the drop of a hat. Maître d' Frank Shane was one of many friends out front who were giving me a boost—and sometimes the boost was a generous head count of the customers. In Las Vegas, that's how you're rated. Finally, Baron Hilton and his wife were ringside for several performances. It all added up to a successful run, and Wolford was all smiles as everything went as he had predicted. I was on my way. I had the strange feeling that this was just the beginning of something bigger to come.

And when you're hot, you've got to capitalize on it. I now tried to set the wheels in motion to make my Las Vegas success pay off for my faltering record career. I knew that if I could set the stage for a record with my next season at the Flamingo, either the record would be helped or my show would. They would

18

tie in. So I began examining where I had come from, and where I was going, on the turntable.

There's no explaining where ideas come from for records, for songs. To have a gold record, a million-plus seller, you've got to capture the imagination of a whole cross section of the American public. Nobody knows why a million or more people will plunk down a dollar or two for a disc. My theory is that to stand out you've got to avoid the fads of the moment. I remembered what columnist Bob Thomas had written about me at the start of my recording days: "Bobby went against the trend among pop singers: he is not Italian and not from South Philadelphia. He is of Polish descent and hails from the same community that spawned Perry Como. Like his fellow townsman, he sings slower, and that also goes against the trend."

An incident now occurred that pushed me in a definite direction in my search for new life in my recording career. Like other entertainers at the gambling spas, I had sometimes "worked free" because of the voracious appetite of the gambling tables. This time, a friend recommended a real estate agent, who would find an investment for me.

Most of the pictures you see of Las Vegas are either indoors or along a single glittering street—the Strip. Go a few blocks in either direction and you'll likely find sand and sagebrush, more familiar to the natives. But my real estate friend pointed out that business was booming and a little plot of land might be in the path of the marching rows of casinos. He showed me something the size of a city lot.

"How much is that?" I asked skeptically.

"Only fifty thousand dollars. Could go to a hundred in a few years. It's the best investment for you, Bobby."

I kicked a clod of earth and watched the sand spiral away in the brisk breezes of the afternoon. Where I come from, this was desert. No trees, no water, no view. Fifty thousand dollars, I thought. For what? If it doubled in a couple of years, so what? It seemed to me that a better investment was myself. Literally. Then and there I decided to spend some money on a song instead of on sand and sagebrush.

But in real life, ideas don't come the way they do in the movies. Composers don't plop down at the piano, start tinkering around, and come up with music and lyrics to "September Song" on the spot. Thoughts come from one corner of your mind, ideas tucked away for future reference come out of your files, and flashes come in the middle of the night. Sometimes suggestions trickle together like streams feeding a river, until suddenly the rivulet becomes a torrent. And then you say, "That's it!"

There was a rivulet flowing through my life at this time that had its source somewhere back in my childhood. I had become aware of being Polish, and proud of it, and vocal about it—just because it told me something about myself. The Vinton name had lost a few letters at the end, somewhere along the line, but it was as Polish a name as anything in Hamtramck, Michigan. My hometown, Canonsburg, Pennsylvania, had a large Polish population. I went to the Polish parochial school for eight years and grew up thinking the whole world was Polish. But I really learned about my ethnic roots from my grandmother, who lived just down the street and provided my home away from home—the place I would run away to, with my wagon, when I ran away from home. She taught me the language and the customs of the old country. I have always gone back to her in my thoughts when I was searching for a new direction in my life.

As I rose in the popular music field I didn't mind letting people know my background, because that was part of *me*. On the other hand, I didn't employ that heritage—not even in the way Perry Como, Jerry Vale, Jimmy Rosselli, and others used Italian themes, nor in the way international figures like Maurice Chevalier and Marlene Dietrich so naturally expressed theirs. In the early seventies, though, a cruel thing was happening that threw a different light on everything. The pattern goes back a long way. First there were the Pat and Mike jokes, making fun of the Irish immigrants. Then the mantle fell to the Swedes—and it was supposedly innocent humor to talk about a big dumb Swede. There were Negro jokes, when Negro wasn't "Black" yet. Finally the Italians and the Poles became the butt of a peculiar type of ridicule. Kids came home from school with the latest Polish joke. I'm sure many of these kids didn't even know what they were repeating. But it was the "in" thing to have the latest one-liner, and it was poisoning children's unformed attitudes drop by drop.

And people like me went along with it! I was

naïve enough to think it was good-natured humor. I was optimistic enough to think those nasty little lines would go away by themselves.

Strangely enough, being in show business made me somewhat immune to this type of humor. I was supposed to go along with gags when I worked with comedians. I wasn't bothered by being the butt of ethnic jokes, but I began to see that the Polish community *was*. I went along when Merv Griffin asked me to join in a theme show with other entertainers of Polish extraction, such as Gloria Swanson, Ted Knight, and Loretta Swit. Merv's idea was that by standing up and talking about the problem we would dissipate it. Shortly after the show was aired the letters started coming in.

"You could have done more," one woman wrote. "You had a chance to speak up and you let it slip by."

Another raised a broader issue: "We don't have any Anti-Defamation League, and this isn't humor—it's prejudice!"

I knew I had to do something to show my fellow Poles that I cared and that I, too, was proud to be Polish.

And then another stream joined the river. I had always loved polkas, but in the music fads of the day there wasn't room for them except in special markets. I had sung in Italian and made records at the San Remo Music Festival. I not only sang in Spanish but was the leading English-speaking male vocalist in some countries of South America. And when I sang in Greek or French or Hebrew or German it wasn't a gimmick—I had learned the basic words of those languages, not in a recording studio, but on the street where I grew up. But I would always ham it up and throw it away when I came to the polkas, the Polish section of my show. And that upset my mother.

"You sing in every language but your own," she would pout—and there's nothing worse than a Polish mother pouting! I tried to explain that there weren't any melodies in Polish that sing well in English. "Then write one yourself!" she pleaded again and again. "The Polish people will love you forever!"

Each concert I gave added further tributaries to the river of my imagination. I had taken the simplest and most beautiful words in any language, "I love you," and put them in Polish with some lyrics that had been at the back of my mind for a long time. The words expressed the pain of a lost love. And one evening, at the Palmer House in Chicago, when a good-natured fan shouted, "How about a Polish song?" I had my chance to give the song a preview. As I launched into the words I had just written, "Moja droga . . ." an electric current surged through the room. The usually sedate Palmer House audience began clapping their hands and stomping their feet along with me, and I could scarcely finish the song. I had my answer: you didn't have to know what the words meant to realize the song had magic. And that's what music is all about.

My mind was now made up. Instead of investing in sand and sagebrush, I would produce the song with the Polish words, "My Melody of Love." I believe everything is timing—doing the right things with the right people at the right time. It was the right time to go back not only to my ethnic roots but to my recording roots. It was the right time to be with Bob Morgan again.

Bob had been my producer at Epic Records when I had my first hits. I remember that he had dropped out of the business to go into something less ulcerous. When I reached him at his home in New York, I discovered he was, ironically, in real estate. "Look, Bob," I said, "we're both out of the business. I'm playing tennis and you're selling real estate. I want you to be with me again, to produce my records like you used to." I took all the money I had, brought him out to California, and set up a rigid schedule of writing and looking for new material and working in the recording studios. After six weeks we had recorded enough sides for an album, and most important, we had something different, something that had a meaning for me—my Polish song. Morgan and I both thought that since I was a little cold in the recording business we should come out first with a song called "Dick and Jane." It was a different idea for a song—it had the little boy inside me singing with me in duet. We figured it would break the ice and make it easy for the Polish song. But the interest at Capitol fizzled out. I knew that "My Melody of Love" had to come next.

It was now Bobby Vinton, salesman, packing his records under his arm and knocking on doors as I did as a kid in Canonsburg, Pa. I sent "My Melody of Love" to my previous record company, Epic. They had the most to gain from a successful record of mine, since they owned my catalog of about forty albums and

24

any hit always helps sell the rest. I would give them first chance. When I received no reply after several weeks had gone by, I had to assume their answer was no. So I went down the line to the other seven major companies: RCA, Capitol, United Artists, and the rest. One by one they had the same answer for me. "Bobby, it's the biggest Polish joke of all—only nobody's going to laugh." All seven said, in one way or another, that they didn't think it had hit potential when they saw the title and the vocalist—and when they heard the words in Polish they were *sure*. If they ever had any interest in signing me as a recording artist, they were now convinced that I was totally unaware of what was going on in the record industry.

This time, I thought, I had gambled and lost. The largest record companies in the country are supposed to know what the public will buy. And logically they were right. Turn a recent graduate of Harvard Business School loose on this assignment, and he'll prove to you it doesn't make economic sense. Sure, someone with Polish pride might wander into a record store and reaffirm his or her allegiance by buying my record. But the Poles with ethnic spirit are just not the type of youngsters who listen to the top twenty. One by one, seven leading record companies shook their mathematical heads on "My Melody of Love."

I had invested all the money I had loose to get back in the swing of the recording business, and, unfortunately, I had lost. I was just about convinced that this was the end of that career, and that I'd better concentrate on my show-business act, when another figure from my past loomed on the horizon.

25

Al and Grace Gallico had been good friends of the Vinton family since my early days in the recording business. They both brought good luck to me as well as good advice. Grace had been a backup singer for Vaughn Monroe when he made his big hit, "There I've Said It Again," and that same song turned out to be a gold record for me. Al is one of the biggest music publishers in the business—it's his job to find songs and songwriters for performers. He's the kind of guy who'll find the right song for you even if he doesn't own the song. When I was making an album in Nashville with a "blue" theme, he handed his secretary a dollar and told her to go out and buy the lead sheet—the piano part—for "Blue Velvet." It wasn't his song, but he knew what would work for me—and it was another gold record. Here I was again at a crossroads, when Al and Grace came over to our house in Southern California for a strictly social visit.

As we squinted lazily into the summer sun setting over Santa Monica bay, the world seemed too peaceful for any talk of business. But the inevitable question came up: What was new with me? "Not much, Al," I said, "I guess Polish isn't *in* this year."

"Tell me about it," he said laughing. And I did, down to the seven turndowns. But he wanted to hear the record anyway. That's what happens when you're a pro. You don't go by the numbers but by the seat of your pants. It was seven to nothing, but the game was just beginning for Al. He said immediately, "I can't believe your own record company turned that down! Who listened to it at Epic?"

I had to answer I honestly didn't know if anyone

had heard it. I had mailed it to them. Al called the company without hesitation and buttonholed the top man. "Have you heard 'My Melody of Love'?" he demanded. "Well, then get it and play it right now. I'm not hanging up until you've heard it." The familiar song wafted to my ears. Then the voice on the other end of the line said, "Hey, what's he singing? I can't make out the words."

"That's Polish," Al explained.

"You've gotta be kidding!" The man at Epic laughed. "Forget it!" And he hung up as if he had just been the victim of an April fool's gag.

Al thought for a minute. "There's one guy you didn't go to who has a good ear," he said. "Jay Lasker. At ABC. I'm taking it over there in the morning." I should have known it before: when you believe in something strongly enough you show it off in person. When a record comes to me fourth-class I don't even open the envelope. You have to make your property as valuable to yourself as you want it to be to the other guy. Perhaps it was because Al Gallico spun "My Melody of Love" in person for Jay Lasker. Perhaps Jay would have eventually seen the merit of the song unaided. In any case, the Polish Prince was born in that meeting. And that's the story I want to tell: the before and after, the dreams of a young man struggling to find himself, the discovery that anyone can do something bigger than himself—even with a song.

Two
The Pennsylvania Kid
or The Heartland

Start from Canonsburg, Pennsylvania, and look in any direction for five hundred miles. That's the heartland I came from and belong to. And because I've got Canonsburg in my veins I can tell when I'm at home. I like that settled way of life, I like families, I like people who work with their hands. I like people who go out to other people, and when I go out on a stage I like the way they come to me—and that's my act.

What could be more American than to grow up on a street named Smith in a town of fifteen thousand people, with good and bad on both sides of the track? I was lucky to have that hometown. I was lucky to grow up in a home my father bought for something like $2,400. From the very beginning I wasn't distracted by the material side of life—away from such basic things as the love of a mother and a father. I often hear entertainers talk about how rough times were when they were growing up. But who *hasn't* had hard times? As they were for many other people, hard times were a way of life for me, and they weren't so hard because they were the only life I knew. We always ate well, played well, and laughed well. The laughter, in fact, could have come only from the very simple life we shared.

The simplicity of the heating system in our house has always been etched in my mind, for a curious reason. The upstairs rooms had vents in the floor, which would be opened to allow heat to come up from below. That was the upstairs heat. You could look down through those vents and spy on the rooms below—a small boy's idea of intrigue and mystery. I guess I was about five years old when I became aware that my father's band would practice downstairs in the evenings when I was supposed to be upstairs asleep. By flattening my head against the wall I could peek down the vents and see a good part of the front room, a collection of strange-looking instruments, and the tops of eight or ten heads. One particular evening, as I watched the rehearsal long into the night, I suddenly realized I had to go to the bathroom, which was downstairs. I was afraid to interrupt my father, and I was equally afraid I couldn't hold out much longer. I solved this dilemma in typical small-boy fashion by peeing on the head of the drummer. Lloyd Morales, my current drummer and long-time friend, says I've been doing the same thing ever since.

As an only child, I must have been spoiled. But

perhaps that wasn't such a bad thing; I knew I was special to my mother and father, and I think I unconsciously tried to do something special with my life. In any case, my father took me everywhere, as far as the car would carry us on the money he had in his pocket. Before he was plucked off by my mother, I'm told he was a dashing young man with the flashiest car in town. His nickname was "Showboat" for that reason, and when I was growing up his friends would call him by that name as casually as they would call him "Stanley," his given name. Stanley Vinton, *Jr.*, was my proud Polish name.

It was inevitable that music would come into my life because, along with being Polish and a traveling man, my father had a band that was the focus of his life. When I was nine years old I had broken a leg diving over a fence, and had to wear a heavy cast for several weeks. But my father had promised to take me to see and hear Les Brown and his "band of renown," so I wound up riding on his shoulders to that dance, at Westview Park in Pittsburgh. Standing near the bandstand, we wore big grins from ear to ear as that big-band sound swelled around us. It was a magic moment. To this day, I'll look out into the audience every now and then at one of my shows and see a young boy sitting there with his father, and I'll see them grinning, and see my father and myself. And these are the moments when I take myself a little more seriously as a musician and an entertainer.

My father's band played at top ballrooms and country clubs, and before long I felt I was a natural part of that side of his life. It started as early as the age of four or five when, at the urging of my mother, I was given a chance to sing at a wedding. It was at the Elks Club in Washington, Pennsylvania, and there I was, decked out in a Little Lord Fauntleroy suit, complete with blue velvet trousers, singing "Playmates, come out and play with me, and bring your dollies three . . . ." I knew the words from having heard it on the radio and in the band's rehearsals, but I unexpectedly added a dimension of my own. After three bars I developed a bad case of the hiccups, which I fought bravely through to the end. To my surprise, I received a shower of pennies, nickels, and dimes—my first paid performance. More than thirty years later, I induced one of *my* children, Kristin, to sing with me—at the Waldorf Astoria in New York City. She sang "Daddy's Little Girl" and naturally stole the show, getting raves from Earl Wilson in his column the next morning. I should have known that there's no act like a kid's act. . . .

Even though I was encouraged in music by my mother and father, I wasn't a prodigy and, in fact, I had to be bribed at the rate of twenty-five cents an hour to practice the clarinet. I thank them to this day for that form of payola. By the standards of child psychologists, something terrible may have happened to me from being paid to play, but musically I know the result was commendable. I became familiar with a great variety of instruments at an early age, whether I was pushed or not. Sometimes I think that the money wasn't as much an inducement as the constant impression on my young mind of bandstands and instruments around the house at all hours of the day, and of a

31

father who wrote arrangements for the band in the back of his truck on his lunch hour.

What fascinated me most were those squiggles on ruled paper that the men in the band somehow translated into blaring trumpet calls, pulsating bass notes, and a cascade of piano chords. I watched my father sketch in the lines with the big black dots at the bottom, pause to sound a few notes, and then erase and add more squiggles. Without him knowing, I decided to lend him a helping hand. I did a little erasing and drawing of my own one day, so neatly, I thought, that my squiggles matched his perfectly.

Soon after, when the band was rehearsing, some strange sounds greeted my father's ears. "Why don't you play what's written?" he yelled. So they played it a second time, and it was still all wrong. Finally my father looked at the score and realized that someone had tried to do a little arranging of his own. He quickly taught me that there was more to writing music than drawing little dots on paper.

"I only wanted to help," I apologized with an impish look.

"Well, next time tell me and maybe we can work together."

"Daddy . . ."

"Yes?"

"Did the band like my notes?"

Maybe I wasn't so innocent. I still get a laugh when I picture the band looking up in bewilderment at my father, and him looking aghast at them. My entire childhood, it seems, was filled with the practical jokes and outlandish adventures of a Polish Tom

Sawyer. The parochial school I attended, St. Genevieve's, was a four-room basement of a church, with two grades in each room. We had to go to the coal room for a drink of water, and the bathrooms were in an outhouse, where, in the winter, we would pee on the floor to make ice for skating. There were ample opportunities for us scalliwags to create havoc for the girls, for the parents, and for the good nuns.

In towns like Canonsburg, where being Polish was almost equivalent to being Catholic, the school was known as the Polish school. For those first eight years of formal education, I thought the whole world was Polish, and indeed Polish was taught right along with English as a matter of course. But for a curious reason—the eagerness of my mother in wanting me to "get ahead"—I learned more about my ethnic background and the only Polish language I have today *out of school* rather than in it. I was put into first grade about two years ahead of my time. All during school days, even into high school, I was in that bewildered state of having to catch up with my buddies. At one point my father had to ask the nuns to take me out of Polish language classes just to give me a breather. I think he knew where I would get a full grounding in everything Polish.

Just a few doors down the street from us lived my mother's parents, Casper and Blanche Studgenski. When I felt the need, as all youngsters do at some point, to run away from home, I would pull my wagon over to "Ba's" place. And because they were so near and so young for grandparents, the Studgenskis were almost another set of parents for me. I relished the

33

kielbasa and klusky—sausage and potato balls—that always seemed to be on the table. And I learned to speak Polish the way a child learns his native tongue, not out of the grammar books. It didn't cross my mind that the first name of my best friend all through grammar school, Edju Rehonic, was simply the Polish form of Edward.

Not surprisingly, the things that stand out in my mind about grammar school days have nothing to do with show business—that is, with the business or the game of entertaining people. Edju and Junior Vinton always managed to become involved in school activities more than in studies. We went to the movies every day, but school *did* interest us. We sang in the school choir under the watchful eye of Sister Modesta; to this day I find it quite natural to bring a religious-oriented song into even a Las Vegas act. I watched how the nuns conducted their annual bazaar to raise funds for the school, and in particular how one shrewd sister greased a plate floating in a tub of water so none of the pennies being pitched at it would stay in the winner's circle. And so I set up carnivals in my own backyard, with all sorts of games to play for pennies, with prizes garnered from my mother's household discards—ashtrays, statues, trinkets. Three black girls, the Bush sisters, were my best customers; integration is the natural state of life for youngsters, especially in a town like Canonsburg. Edju and I climaxed our show-business career in the eighth grade at a play to celebrate the twenty-fifth anniversary of our pastor's ordination. As Father Szelong watched with ill-concealed amusement, two boys dressed as wise old

34

owls unintentionally fell from the top tier of a set of animals, sending cats and dogs and other costumed children scattering across the stage. They were Edju and me.

It was quite natural for us to continue in the same direction in high school. Whenever there was an opportunity to participate in a class play or minstrel show, we were there. And when I marched in the school band, I found a way to sneak Edju in, carrying a tuba and pretending to play it. Little by little, we began to take things more seriously. I was elected president of the drama club. I began to believe that if everybody had to find a niche for himself in life, mine would be in the entertainment field. Then something happened that sent me on my way.

It seemed to be one of those scenes that are destined to be the opening sequence of a movie. I was playing football and chased an errant punt off the field. When I finally picked the ball up, I found myself in front of a side door of the Eagles Hall. I heard what sounded like one of the big bands my father had taken me to see. As I stared dreamily in the door, I saw high school chums Joe Dybell, Tony Luchetti, John Milick, Mickey Mazza, Jim Bell—just kids like me—creating the sound of a real orchestra. It was a revelation. It may sound presumptuous for a fourteen-year-old kid in Canonsburg, but I actually thought to myself that this was a perfect scene, this is where the movie would begin, if the story of my life were ever done. I knew then that what I wanted to do with my life was to make a mark in the popular music field; if they could form a band and play like that, so could I.

Joe Dybell had walked into grammar school with me on the very first day. We had walked into high school together. He would one day be the best man at my wedding, and I at his. To see him playing there in the Eagles Hall was almost to see myself. And in a matter of days, the dream began to become real. Four kids my age, who stuck together because they were from a close-knit Greek background, came to me with an offer I couldn't refuse. Your father is a bandleader, they said. If you can help get the instruments and the bandstands and some arrangements, we'll form a band of our own and make you the leader. And so Carl, George, Greggy, and "Buttercup," who later would make their fame and fortune as the "Four Coins," teamed up with me in a Greek "kids" band. It wasn't long before Joe Dybell and some other friends of mine came over to our aggregation—and my father couldn't have been more pleased.

For a while, of course, we weren't ready to play a full-fledged date. But the Stanley Vinton *Junior* band had the advantage of being able to use the Greek Hall for rehearsal. I remember it had no heat, so we'd have to light the stoves in the kitchen and sit on them while we played. And we began to play at Greek weddings and other functions. As the leader, I had to handle the financial arrangements, and it always seemed to me that the Greeks had a strange way of counting, even though the money came out right in the end. The important thing wasn't the money, but that music was becoming the focus of our lives. In particular, I didn't feel the need to go along with the usual teen-age routines, such as dating, nor did my parents find it strange that I wasn't bringing girls home. For one thing, I was young for my class; for another, there weren't those peer pressures and expectations of parents that often force kids into roles as they do in today's society. I was a wiry kid, still growing: I could make the weight for the eighty-eight-pound team in high school wrestling.

Oh, but appearances are deceptive! Although I had my own band, I was now proficient enough to play in my father's. And on big dates, such as a New Year's Eve dance, he needed all the brass he could lay his hands on. We were playing on such an occasion at a club called Ianetti's, in Steubenville, Ohio, when another big push was given to my direction in life. The bar was right up next to the bandstand, and as the magic moment of midnight approached, the revelers were really whooping it up. The dancers were swirling by, requesting their favorite numbers, and the women in particular were winking and whistling their appreciation. As the horns went off at midnight, one buxom young lady jumped up on the platform and began showering the band and me with kisses. I was grinning from ear to ear, but her husband wasn't amused. The bartender, a roly-poly type with a wide white apron, jumped in between us. "Now, everybody take it easy," he admonished.

"This guy's trying to make out with my wife and I don't care if it *is* New Year's Eve—I'm going to wipe that smile off his face!"

The bartender spread his arms wide. "Look, mister—he's just a kid. He's only fifteen years old!"

"He's *shit* just a kid!" As I ducked behind the

bartender's apron I thought to myself, Now, *there's* a compliment! It was another scene from my secret movie—it was the first time I began kissing as a part of my performance, although I didn't realize till much later what a friendly way this was to warm up an audience. It was beginning to dawn on me: entertaining is like making love.

And somewhere there's a stripper named Suzie who had me pegged from the very beginning. One of the first engagements our band got was to play backup music for the main act at a VFW club in Burgettstown, Pennsylvania. Remember, I was still "just a kid"—my Uncle Ziggy had to drive me to the place. Suzie's gimmick was to unveil a level of clothing as we played each verse of "If You Knew Suzie." I had strict instructions to stop after three verses, because that's as far as she was going to go. Naturally, I couldn't resist going on—to four verses, and then to five. By this time Joe Dybell, who was playing trumpet in the back row and was standing up to get a better view, had to sit down with a red face. A very flustered Suzie ended her act by walking off in a huff—and the foot-stomping crowd loved it. It suddenly occurred to me that they thought it was part of the act! Backstage, Suzie chided me. "I don't know who you are, young man," she said, "but when you grow up you're going to be a dirty old man!"

One of the adults who guided us through those heady, devil-may-care years was Miss Scroggs, our English teacher. We often played weddings on Saturday nights and for other family affairs on Sunday, and would wind up packing our instruments home in the early dawn of Monday. She knew we were burning the candle at both ends, but with the sensitivity that went beyond being a teacher she was tolerant of our drooping eyes. School hadn't failed us; among the members in our band I was perhaps the only one who didn't have a definite career mapped out. Joe Dybell was intent on becoming an engineer. Chuck Cochran knew he had a career as a musician. He could take a Billy May or a Stan Kenton record and dash down all the parts by stopping the record every so often—his pitch was that good. Riding to an engagement in the car with us, he'd shout out, "Hey, listen to that train—E flat." A talent like that is all the more remarkable when you consider he was only fifteen; when we played in my father's band, we would be playing marbles on our break. Chuck, by the way, lives in Nashville and recently wrote the arrangement for "Don't It Make My Brown Eyes Blue," a big record by Crystal Gayle.

And then there was another old buddy of mine since grammar school days, John "Speedy" Thomas, who kept hanging around our rehearsals, trying to break in with us with a singing group. And this was another of those little accidents that would bring me back again to my Polish heritage. His quartet, the Pacemakers, loosely modeled on the currently hot Four Aces, was a challenge to the Greeks who had originally talked me into forming the band. Buttercup and his crew wouldn't take it lying down. Hey, they said, we can sing as good as they can, as well as play in the band. And soon they were singing so well that they began to get ideas about going their own way.

"Who's going to listen to four singers on a record?" I argued. But they were good, and the public was in the mood for their tight-harmony style. They dubbed themselves the Four Coins, and went off to seek their fortune in New York. All of a sudden, I had lost my connection with the Greeks—the weddings at seventy-five dollars a night, split eight ways, and especially the Greek Hall for rehearsals. But where could we practice? The Polish Hall, of course!

I walked into the Polish Falcons Hall and spelled out my proposition to the bartender. If my band could rehearse there on Monday nights, we'd give them a free dance for any of their special events. He looked at my cherubic sixteen-year-old face and shook his head. "What band? We don't want no kids in here."

"C'mon," I answered, "look at the money you'll save. And besides, it's classy to have music playing in the background—good for the bar." The following Monday we were upstairs rehearsing, and it soon became familiar to hear our music wafting out across the east end of Canonsburg on warm summer evenings. It was another scene for the movie—the tough bartender backing down to the eager young kid—and there in the background, visible only to me in my subconscious, was a large eagle, the Polish national symbol, staring down at me from the back bar. One day it would be emblazoned across my chest on a Polish Power T-shirt, or on the back of my jacket as I sang for twenty thousand people in an auditorium in Chicago.

But my first professional appearance, before a group of people who came just to hear the band, was still ahead of me. It finally came time to give a free dance for the members of the club and anyone else who wished to attend. We were well rehearsed; we had the latest big-band sounds down to a T. We placed announcements around town and notified our buddies. But when the fateful evening came, an hour went by without anyone coming upstairs to the dance hall. I went down to the bar and asked sheepishly if we had the right night. Finally two people showed up—my aunt Mary Fish and my grandmother "Ba." The two ladies sat quietly while we went through our renditions of the latest Stan Kenton hits, but all they did was frown at the high trumpets. Finally they began calling, between numbers, "Play polka! Play polka!" As they were about to leave, I relented and "rolled out the barrel." They got up and danced around the room with each other as if the music would never stop. Two drunks came up the stairs, watched the spectacle for several minutes, looked at each other in astonishment, and quickly retreated to the bar. As disastrous as it may sound, everyone had a great time, even the band, and it must have lodged in my mind that there was something in my Polish soul that refused to be denied.

At least I knew that there was nowhere to go but up. If I felt I was floundering in school, if I didn't know exactly what I was going to do with my life, at the same time I had the strong feeling that I was going to accomplish something substantial. Sometimes you have to go to the bottom of the well to see the stars.

The Greeks got a big laugh out of our fiasco at the Polish Hall. I was about as far from being a Polish prince as one can be. But little by little, things began

41

to fall into place. I was beginning to learn that I had to get to know the older, more experienced people in my business. Every Wednesday night, I knew, the musicians' union gave a free dance for the teen-agers in the community. I convinced the officials who made the decisions that there was no reason why my band couldn't give those free performances, free, that is, to the dancers. There were some union funds to pay the orchestra. So one Wednesday evening, the young dancers looked up and saw someone their own age instead of their seniors. We were an instant hit. All of a sudden, at this dance at Eagles Hall, I discovered that people *want* to have fun, and want the performer to succeed. It was a brand-new world; I felt I was at a party, the center of attention, doing something I dearly wanted to do, and getting paid for it!

Our Polish band even began to attract a following, and a young lady began to move into my life as a kind of unofficial fan club president. I had first noticed her in grammar school, and thought of her for a long while as the girl with no eyelashes, because at our first meeting she had been singed over a stove in an accident. I played for her graduation; we danced a little and then I rejoined the band for the engagement! Speedy, who lived next door to Dolly Dobbin, said to me, "What do you want to take her out for? She's still got her morals."

Dolly's family lived in a rather rough neighborhood, which was known as the "Patch"—something like a company town for the mining workers of Canonsburg. The Irish as well as the Poles were definite minorities here. I recall once seeing Dolly chasing a big black boy with a baseball bat: there, I thought, is a woman who can take care of herself! Mining, and tragedy, forged a kind of link between our families. On the day her grandfather was to retire, at the age of sixty-five, he was killed in a cave-in. And my paternal grandfather, who was Lithuanian-Polish and gave the name Vinton to us, was also killed in a coal-mine accident. My father told me how, at the age of five, he saw his father carried home in a blanket by his fellow workers and laid out on the floor. There was no ambulance, no hospital, no nurse. Dolly's father narrowly survived a prisoner-of-war camp in the Second World War. And my aunt Mary Fish, who danced so proudly at my first public performance, would later see her son off for Vietnam from California, then, returning to Canonsburg, be killed in a commercial airline crash.

We always say these are the things that happen only to other, anonymous people. I learned from an early age that they don't. With the end of high school I was to leave Canonsburg and seek my way in the bigger, unknown world, first stop Duquesne University. I was bringing more than academic credentials with me. Our orchestra was well on the way to success. Before I left Canonsburg, I was even vying with my father as a bandleader. People would call the house, asking for the Stanley Vinton band, and my mother wouldn't know which of us they wanted. Finally my father said, "One of us is going to have to change his name, and it isn't going to be me."

So I took my confirmation name, Robert, as my professional first name. That was a bandleader's name! I had made a break with my past—or had I? At any rate, there weren't any Bobbys in my hometown.

43

THREE
The Farther
Out of Town You Go,
the Bigger You Are

Not too long ago, a woman asked to come backstage after one of my shows and introduce herself. She had a familiar name and said she knew me in high school. But I would never have recognized her under all the makeup and extra pounds. I could almost hear the guys in the band saying, "You knew *her* in high school?" We exchanged some friendly words, and she said good-bye with this parting shot: "You know, Bobby, if I knew you were going to be a great star back when we were in school together, I would have dated you."

That incident pretty well sums up what happens to those who seek fame and fortune—in the eyes of their friends who "knew them when." When you've "made it," everyone still wants to think of you as you once were. And when you're just starting out, it can be a great handicap to have to depend on your hometown supporters. Don't do it. Get out of town as fast as you can.

With the end of high school, the Bobby Vinton band had to dissolve, as many of us went our separate ways. But it quickly re-formed as a college band, with Joe Dybell and Chuck Cochran still with me, and newcomers like Jim Drake and Bob McCoy signing on. The "BV" band started to move out to a bigger pond—specifically the "tristate" area from Steubenville, Ohio, to Pittsburgh, to Weirton and Wheeling, West Virginia. We were making money to help support our college expenses, but most of all, we were gaining valuable experience as professionals.

It soon became apparent to my father that *my* Vinton band was the wave of the future. His kind of music was still great for weddings and the more conservative dances, but the young people, who were looming ever larger as the main force in the entertainment market, wanted something more in step with the times. We decided to merge little by little, as he played in my band and I played in his, and by the time my college band was on the move he brought his best players over to me and told me to take the baton. He would be the manager. And since I still looked boyish—I was only seventeen when I entered college—he would be my front when we had to impress someone. When we went into a hall to perform, he would walk ahead of me. The dance organizers were assured that here was a solid, well-established organization!

Stanley Vinton, Sr., knew well the importance of

45

appearance and bearing and planning. True to his nickname, "Showboat," he wouldn't think of making a business call without shoes shined and every hair in place. (That may have gone out of style for many years, but it still applies and I think the successful performers today are the first to admit it.) And he knew what it took to line up work consistently. We'd scan the newspapers for announcements. "Mrs. James White of Steubenville is in charge of arrangements for the dance," an item would read. We'd find out when and where the dance was to be held. We'd look for weddings, coming-out parties, affairs of all kinds. And then we'd string an itinerary between them. My eyes were opened: the farther you had to travel to a performance date, the more you were appreciated. You were like imported wine.

We needed printed cards, with our photo and a full description of our organization, to send out to prospective customers. We now had matching jackets, "BV" bandstands, and eleven pieces. Now, every band of that time was supposed to have a lead singer—so I persuaded my mother to pose in our picture as our vocalist. At a time when most kids are going through some kind of withdrawal symptoms from their parents, here I was with a father playing saxophone for me and a mother posing in a full-length gown as I looked on with that knowing smile of the bandleader. To make everything complete, she helped pay for printing the cards.

One of the pleasant side effects of having a family band was that we stayed together as a family in other ways, too. The greatest compliment I received in my early days was being identified with my father. One evening a trumpet player became unruly after a little too much to drink and refused to listen to my father's corrections. "You and your old man make me sick," he shouted at me. "I quit!" I was the bandleader, but everyone knew the two of us thought alike. And we were also very much alike in our stubbornness.

Intense feelings existed between us over our tastes in popular music, and, though they seldom came to the surface, when they did, a volcano erupted. At a dance in Weirton, W.Va., my father leaned over and whispered halfway through, "Make the next one a polka." As I said, "Not now," my father's face started to turn red. I turned to the mike as the song was ending and announced, "Now, by popular demand—a number to describe our saxophone section, entitled after them . . . 'Bewitched, Bothered, and Bewildered.'" As I said each word of the title, I pointed in turn to our three saxophonists, Al Sprando, Tony Lucchitti, and my dad. I expected a reaction, but not what followed. Dropping his saxophone, my father pushed his way through flying sheet music and falling music stands and tore up the polka music. We wrestled to the floor of the bandstand as the music played on. The crowd kept dancing: Wow! They really carry their gags a long way!

"Wait a minute, Dad!" I howled. But this time he was serious.

"So you're the bandleader, huh? Well, listen to this. You can't have the car for a week. Wait till we get home, 'cause there I'm the boss!" And he was.

We dusted ourselves off, and smiled sheepishly at the dancers.

Little by little, the polkas came into our repertoire. For the rest of his short life, he would be, in one way or another, a sharer in my musical career as well as in my life. But for the moment, he was the strength in the band, and I was the gimmick—"the young man with a band." And my mother was the prodder. "Do it now, while you're young!" was her constant advice whenever I had to make a career decision.

College may not have done much for me academically, but it opened up other directions in music for me—and that alone was enough to justify it. Some of us were invited to play along with members of the Pittsburgh Symphony in a special students' performance. I played the oboe and considered seriously taking it up as a profession. I was also able to fill in the gaps in my knowledge of musical composition. I learned a lesson that has always remained with me: write everything simple, so any practiced musicians can play it at sight.

Our band was still making that trip down to the Polish Falcons Hall in Canonsburg to practice, and they groaned about that twenty-five-mile trip on a school night. Then we joined the musicians' union in Pittsburgh, where we could rehearse, and we were soon accepted as full professionals. We began to line up jobs as backup band for major entertainers who came to Pittsburgh. I remember especially the evening Sammy Davis, Jr., performed in front of us.

When we started playing, Sammy turned around and did a double-take. "Who *is* that trumpet player?" he said in astonishment. He was talking about Bob McCoy; he didn't expect to hear that kind of playing from the Bobby Vinton kid band. And Bob went on to the top of his business, where he is today.

Players came and went, but a few fast friends like Jim Drake kept the nucleus of the band intact through the college years and after. I think the big reason we stayed together through tough times was that we were so close together in personality and background and aspirations that we thought alike. We knew what was good for the band as a whole because we knew our strengths and weaknesses.

In one of my college courses, I was to teach young students how to play the oboe. The instructor who was checking on me kept butting in: "That's not the way to do it. First you start from the—"

"Look," I said, "you teach the oboe your way, and I'll teach it the way it's *played.*"

So I became known as something of a rebel in college. What I didn't accomplish in grades, I made up for in street wisdom. I wanted to broaden my knowledge of the whole entertainment business, so I developed a second interest that would involve me in nightclub shows as well as orchestra work. At Duquesne I got together with a singer, Mike Lazo, and a comedian, Gene Schachter, and said, in effect, "Let's see what happens. I'll play the instruments, you'll do your solos, and we'll sing together in between." It was the only way we could break into the clubs around Pittsburgh—and it worked.

In a sense, the two sides of my show-business life worked all too well. The Hi-lites, as we first called ourselves—later, the Tempos—were a hit at clubs like the Bon Ange in Pittsburgh and became as popular as the Bobby Vinton band. Often I would have conflicting dates, and my father would take over the direction of the orchestra. As the pace of the Tempos quickened, I found myself alibiing to the band. Something had to give.

First I leaned to the trio, which had a more exciting future in those days. We took several trips to New York to make demos—demonstration records of our best numbers—and we were all learning the basics of the business: how to deal with agents and where to look for opportunities. We learned the hard way. Once we were approached in the Bon Ange Club by a smooth-looking gentleman, who said we were ready for the big time. He would set us up for a recording session with his company, RCA. We celebrated with champagne and talked up a storm. But when we went to the airport the next morning to accompany him to New York, he was nowhere in sight, and a phone call to New York confirmed that there was no such person at RCA. On another occasion, we auditioned for Arthur Godfrey's "Talent Scouts" show and failed to make the grade—perhaps because we weren't ready, or perhaps because a gentleman with "eggbeater eyebrows" rode up with us in the elevator and sensed we were all laughing at those eyebrows. It turned out he was the producer of the show.

I knew I wasn't putting out 100 percent with the band, and it began to get to me. My father echoed my sentiments and asked me to make up my mind about which way I was going to go. Graduation time was approaching. All of a sudden, the decision was made for me—by the U.S. government. I had to put in my army duty and went off to Fort Knox, Kentucky, for basic training, and then on to Fort Dix, New Jersey. The Tempos got another instrumentalist to fill my spot. Sure enough, as soon as I left town a call came for them to go to New York and make a record. It was good-bye to the band and the club circuit for Bobby Vinton, at least for a while.

The name of the song they recorded, which became one of the biggest hits of that summer, was "See You in September."

FOUR
I Want My Son to Do That for Me Someday

The U.S. Army has a way of bringing reality into a young man's life—fast. "Boys will be boys" isn't part of its rule book. If there was any cockiness instilled in me by being a bandleader in my teens, it was whisked away the first morning a sergeant stood over me and advised me that if I didn't want to get up in the morning there was an alternative called KP. And the second morning and the third morning the "alternative" was increased. Getting up in the morning soon became quite enjoyable by comparison.

Like everybody else, I found a lot of things that were confining and annoying about those first six months of basic training. But my army experience confirmed in me a belief I've always kept with me: there are good sides to everything and there is good in every person. The real challenge isn't to avoid the bad—it's to find the good.

It took a Polish sergeant to show me this truth; by accident or by fate, someone Polish has always played a critical role in my life. Sergeant Kwaczek was that man, when it was time for me to put away the fun and games and set my sights on accomplishing something. He knew instinctively how to handle men to draw out their best efforts. I think he immediately saw a "goofing-off" habit in me that had come from barnstorming with the band. And he worked on finding and encouraging a serious vein in me, of which I was unaware.

The army was also a chance to stand back from my work and evaluate what I was doing in the "real" world. My father was now leading the band in my absence. He had begun to take to the music of the younger generation. Rock and roll was reaching its peak, and we had added something new to it: the big-band sound. Idols of ours like Maynard Ferguson were bringing real instrumental talent to the pop music field. When I hopped the bus home from Fort Dix, it whetted my appetite all the more to pick up where I had left off and do something big with the BV band.

On one of my leaves, I had to explain a bandage on my neck. It was the result of that old habit of getting out of step with the rest of the world. In college, I was sometimes given a passing grade in a course just because the professor wanted to be sure I wouldn't come back. When you do things your own way, you tend to stand out in the crowd, sometimes unfavorably. So it is, only more so, in the army. I became the kind of guy—until I learned better—who is routinely "volunteered" for the dirty work. That's how I wound up on the firing range holding up targets for machine-gun practice.

At first the sound of live ammunition whining overhead is frightening. I thought to myself: Now I know what a deer feels like. But after a short time it becomes another job, in which your chief duty is to keep your head down. In the hot New Jersey sun I had taken my helmet off, then my shirt, and I was well on my way to a great suntan. All of a sudden something seemed to explode right under my chin. The telephone that I was using to call hits and misses back to the gunners was knocked out of my hand. My throat was fiery, and I really thought I was dead. A bullet had ricocheted down the culvert and cut a clean line across the skin of my throat. In that one close call I quickly woke up to the seriousness of following orders, such as keeping a helmet on.

I came back from my short tour in the army a more mature man, and more determined than ever to accomplish something in life. I would lead my band to new heights, or I'd know the reason why not. My research started, silly though it may sound, with a movie. Elvis Presley was just beginning to startle the nation with his hound-dog voice and his shake-a-leg style of performance. At first I didn't quite understand his appeal. But you have to listen to any kind of music, even classical, many times to know enough about it to like it or dislike it. That's the secret of radio and the basic power of disc jockeys. I wanted to know everything I could about "making it" in the big time.

In *Jailhouse Rock*, Presley played the type of performer I had identified with. There he was on the magic silver screen, bigger than life, saying, "We'll make our own records. We'll form our own record company." In words to that effect, he went about recording his song at a studio, slapped on a label, took it around to all the d.j.'s and record stores, and was soon off to the top of the charts. It was as simple as that. If it could be that simple in real life, I said to myself, I'll do it with my band. Why not? I would become a record company executive, even if the only person in the company was me.

With all the savings I had, I cut and pressed a couple of instrumentals featuring the best pieces my band was then doing. I had labels printed up, calling my company, prophetically enough, "Melody Records." I stored everything in my basement, slapping on the labels whenever I had to take a few records around to the stores. The meager sales of the discs weren't enough to repay the costs of recording, but at least I had my hand in the game. And, trudging around Pittsburgh from store to store, I began to get a feel for the business. I was learning the hard way that there's a magic number in this business that's the difference between fame and oblivion: the top twenty.

Then, once again, a Polish man entered my life. I met him in a record store as he was doing the same difficult thing I was: trying to sell an unknown label to a skeptical clerk. He was a large man, on crutches, missing his left leg from the knee down. "Let's see what you've got," he said in a gruff but inviting voice.

I was happy to show my records to anyone who· expressed an interest. This man was sort of a Polish "Colonel Parker"—Elvis's legendary manager and promotion man—to several local singers. By trade he was a gambler; a one-time miner, he had lost his leg in the digging of the Holland Tunnel. We were miles apart in background and appearance, but we shared an almost blind faith in the power of a song. Through a strange symbiotic relationship with each other we became close friends; in fact, the "characters" in my life have always been closer than anyone else. In any event, at that first meeting, he took particular interest in a vocal I had done on the reverse side of one of our instrumentals: "It Was Always in My Heart." As would happen for years afterward, when a tear came into his eye I knew I had a song. It moved him.

My Polish critic—Joe Gorlack was his name— came over to my house regularly to see how I was doing, to play some of his things for me, and to shoot the breeze. He would wave a crutch to my mother and say, "Bob needs me to do his legwork for him," or "I can get my foot in a lot of doors for him." He was the first to tell me I was really a vocalist, and for years afterward he would play a critical, and often funny, role in my life as a singer.

Little by little, I began to discover other cracks in the door of success. From time to time I went back to the Bon Ange Club, where our college trio, the Hilites, had played successfully. It was the type of club you'd see in the movies, where a Jimmy Cagney or a Humphrey Bogart would hang out. There was always some action on basketball scores and big money seemed to pass from hand to hand frequently. The owner of the Bon Ange, Cuddy Albert, loved to sing, and he was a likable guy with a resonant voice. His singing had been one of the reasons he had bought the club; it was his way of eventually getting into show business. Whenever he sang, his boys lining the walls at the back of the room gave him a solid send-off. It occurred to me one day that he was missing a bet.

"Look, Cuddy," I said, "I've got a record label. You can be one of my artists. With all the friends you've got in the industry, you can be on all the jukeboxes in Pittsburgh. One of the safest investments you can make is to cut a record."

"How much up front?" he wanted to know.

"Around $5,000 in all."

"Hell, I can swing that."

"Right. And you'll have something to show for it even if it flops. We'll get it in the stores. We'll get it on the radio. Have we got a deal?" Cuddy shook on it, and I had signed my first artist. I would go to New York, set up a recording session, and he would meet me as soon as everything was ready.

I was riding high—a recording executive off to the Big Apple. But I took a bus, anyway, because my girl Dolly was working at this time as a Greyhound ticket agent and usually had passes for me. In New York I lined up an orchestra, a studio, engineers, and Jim Drake did the arrangement. I even hired a harpist—that was Cuddy's style. But when the big day arrived and Cuddy was nowhere in sight, I began to worry. I called Pittsburgh and found him still there.

"Cuddy," I yelled, "where the devil are you? We've got the band in the studio waiting for you."

"Call it off," he said nonchalantly.

"What! I can't call it off. The money's spent. Get up here!"

"Something's come up we can't talk about over the phone," he said quietly. "They're just bluffing you." He wouldn't budge. I could see that little drawing they do in comic strips—a wad of bills with wings on it flying out the window. The trouble was, I was the one who had signed for everything, including the harpist.

I bused myself back to Pittsburgh with my debut as a recording executive in a shambles. Before I knew what was happening, a summons arrived from the musicians' union. As the responsible party, I would have to come up with the $3,000 or be outlawed by the union. That meant for life. I would never be able to play again anywhere as a member. The union tried to be helpful, but rules were rules. When they suggested that I sue Albert, I had to laugh. The guys around the club had been known to get physical for things a lot less annoying than a lawsuit.

Cuddy's answer to the plight of my career in the union was consistent. "Aw, they're just bluffin' you, kid." I had to do something fast. I didn't want to get my father involved, but the whole thing was soon common knowledge. His reaction was immediate.

"I'll give you the money, son. It's the thing to do." I pleaded with him that he didn't have $3,000. I knew that we made only $20 a night each when the band played; $3,000 seemed like an imaginary number. But he took just about everything out of his modest savings and insisted I take it. I decided to show the same kind of courage he had. If he could wipe out his life's savings just like that, I could bring a claim against Albert for the same amount. I filed my complaint with the union the day I paid the $3,000. His place was then off-limits to union musicians until he repaid me.

Albert was flabbergasted. "Listen, punk—I didn't make any record in New York and I ain't payin' for one."

"Tell it to the union," I shot back. Our case was heard the following week, and I walked in trembling. I was caught between an obligation to my father and wild fears about what Cuddy would do. He showed up with a retinue of friends, big burly types.

"Listen, you chiseler," he greeted me. "Are you gonna go through with this?"

"I don't have any choice," I said. "I borrowed the money from my father, and that's all he's got."

"You sure you know what you're doin'?"

"Yeah, Cuddy. I'd rather have it out with you than let my father down." He stared at me for what seemed like an eternity, then reached into his pocket and counted out a wad of hundreds. "I'll pay," he said at last. "Now let's get outa here."

We stood on the hall's steps, in a circle of his friends. He called me over. "I still don't think I owe you anything, kid," he said quietly. "But I have a son, too. I like what you did for your father. Look, what you just did for him, I hope my son does that for me some day."

59

Five
What Would Happen if Somebody Sang a Song Plain and Straight and Simple?

There's a truism in show business that's been put many ways, but I find this the simplest. Don't make *money* moves—make *career* moves. This came naturally to me as I was searching for a place in records.

Here's an example. Some people will tell you to push for top dollar right at the start—nobody will ever donate it to you. And they will respect you more and place a higher value on your work if you demand big money. This is only part of the story. I've asked for and gotten big fees. Las Vegas is a good example. But that's after I've proved myself in that field. When I made my first try at getting into films, I took a fee that was laughable. I was the star of one of the first of a new and popular type of film—the surf-party movie. I worked for almost nothing because I wanted to open up a new medium for myself. Unfortunately, the movie was popular only with my dog—but that's another story.

When I think of how some performers or businessmen want their money up front, before they've shown they can do anything, I have to shudder. Every good idea I've had, every move that has panned out, has come because I tried to think of *doing* something before getting any pay at all for it. My gradual transformation from a bandleader to a singer came about that way.

One of the discs I had cut on my own label—Melody—was that moody old instrumental that shows off the sax so well, "Harlem Nocturne." I had hustled it around to the d.j.'s in Pittsburgh and had gotten some good air time with it. My best friend at the time, Jim Drake, was responsible for a lot of the work and talent that went into it. Between eating liverwurst sandwiches and apples, which gave him the nickname "Dogbreath," Jim worked as hard as I did on the band—and still found time to handle his studies. Maybe the secret was his diet. In any case, we both had high hopes for that record and didn't pay much attention to what we put on the flip side.

A big disc jockey in Pittsburgh, a fast-talking, savvy guy named Dick Lawrence, played it more as an example of local-kid-makes-good than a piece of musicianship. I stopped in to see him one day to thank him, and he tossed a curve at me. "Why don't you try more singing, Bobby? There's something about your voice on the flip side I like." It was the same thing Joe Gorlack had said.

"The flip side? I was just filling space."

"Yeah, but I can tell you're pushing for something. That's what makes a song sell—the feeling you put into it."

"That's music to my ears," I gulped. "Tell me more!"

"Okay, I will. One of the things that makes a d.j. hang around this business so long is the thought that someday he's going to discover another star. A Presley. A Tony Bennett. A Peggy Lee." Then he came directly to the point. "I say let's go to New York and cut some records."

The Cuddy Albert fiasco was fresh in my mind. I hesitated for a moment, and he read my mind. "Don't worry about money. Just bring some songs and yourself." It was another scene from my secret movie. The heavy guy picks me out of the crowd. "Just bring some songs. . . ." And, I said to myself, don't ask for money up front—this is your opportunity.

I had been composing songs all along. Driving home late at night from engagements, I'd toss lyrics around in my head and practically work out the accompaniment on the spot. And, of course, I had been thinking about Dolly. Many of our dates were at my grandmother's house—"Ba's"—because she had the only piano in the family. It was there I wrote a song called "My First Impression," and Dolly must have been in some way responsible for that. Then I wrote one especially with her in mind: "I Love You the Way You Are." Drake and I hurriedly worked out the arrangements for these two songs, and I flew to New York with Lawrence.

I had only a vague idea of what the financial arrangements for all this were. Lawrence insisted, "Don't worry, I'll handle everything." We went to the recording studio and began working. After about two hours, I could see Lawrence trying to get someone on the phone. I overheard him say, "You've got to see this guy." Pretty soon in walked a good-looking, black-haired gentleman whom everyone seemed to recognize. Lawrence introduced him to me as George Goldner, a small pop record company owner. They went into the control room and we began cutting "I Love You the Way You Are." I could tell from all the nodding and smiling that things were going well.

After the musicians had filed out, the three of us pulled up chairs. Here comes the punch line, I thought. To my surprise, Goldner volunteered an opinion. "You're good, young man. A different style. I think you'll do well with these cuts."

Lawrence nodded. "I knew you'd think so."

"Who's picking up the tab? Who owns the deal?" Goldner asked casually. I got a sinking feeling in my stomach.

"You do. I figured you'd like him."

Goldner looked puzzled, then smiled. "But what if I didn't like him?"

"But you did."

"Dick," Goldner said, "I've got to hand it to you. I'll sign for it." It was all becoming clear. Lawrence had conned the studio and the musicians into thinking Goldner was paying for everything. Then he banked on Goldner wanting the deal. And now he pulled the final rabbit out of the hat. Without a moment's hesitation he turned down Goldner's offer.

"Don't do anything rash," he said. "Let's get together later and talk terms." I didn't have to ask Lawrence why he put Goldner off. As we walked out of the studio he said to me, "If Goldner thinks you're good enough to buy on the spot, I'll pick up the tab and we'll sell you to a *bigger* company."

I don't think that session was ever paid for.

The next day we took our tapes to Columbia and we signed a contract with their subsidiary, Epic. It appeared to me that they were willing to buy the tapes so quickly only because Dick Lawrence was a major d.j. and had played a good many Columbia records in his time. Call it payola if you wish. "You do something for me, I'll do something for you. Nobody gets hurt." That's the street logic. It's a way of life, and always has been, in this country and just about anywhere in the world. It's the reason why a big contributor to a national party expects to receive an appointment as an ambassador if his party wins the election. That's only one example of payola in politics and business—but unfortunately the record industry was singled out as the fall guy by Congress in the fifties. The airwaves were supposed to be public property, and payola there meant somebody was making money off the public. I want to know if the public was hurt by payola—or if the public is hurt even more by what's happened as a reaction to those so-called scandals. Nowadays the radio stations are so afraid of being accused of payola that they restrict the popular music they play to a very select list. The result is that new talent has a harder time than ever reaching the public.

In any case, I was now under an Epic contract,

and the tapes I made were given to Lawrence even though Columbia had paid for them. As we will see, the tape of "I Love You the Way You Are" was to come back to haunt me—though that was the furthest thing from my mind at the time. My contract meant only that I would get a chance to show my stuff. I didn't receive an advance, and any expenses in producing my records would be charged to my account until one or more of my records showed a profit.

My euphoria about being "signed" passed quickly. Our band was making further progress; we got a shot on a program called "TV Talent Scouts." The format of this show involved guest hosts and their discoveries. In our case, Guy Lombardo introduced us as a bright new sound. And the TV exposure led to a contract as a backup orchestra for touring vocalists, such as Fabian and Chubby Checker. We'd pile into buses and go from city to city. It was another scene for my movie, reminiscent of the experience of the big-band era, when the Millers and the Dorseys would hop from one overnight appearance to another up and down the Eastern Seaboard. Only the band wasn't the big attraction, and it began to work on me. We'd file out of the bus, blinking at the crowds, only to discover that the vocalists received all the attention. People would come running up to me and say, "Which one are you?" I would have to say, "I'm not one of the singers—I'm the bandleader." Their answer would be, as they turned away, "Oh. . . ."

It was bad enough that the singers commanded the big paychecks. They also got the girls. "Think of this," I'd say to the girls. "I might be a star someday, and if you get my autograph now you won't have to fight for it then." Every time but once they answered, "When you're a star, we'll fight for it." The exception was a girl in Harrisburg, Pennsylvania. She bought my reasoning, and took my autograph. Five years later, when I was touring with a handful of gold records to my credit, a note came backstage from the same girl. She wanted to show me that old autographed picture.

Once I bribed an usher in one of the theaters we were playing to hand out my photos row by row. They weren't doing me any good in my suitcase. After the show I went to the men's room, and there I saw my photos neatly dumped in the trash can.

Somewhere in the middle of all this I finally got a call from Epic. "Come on up and let's make some records," Jim Fogelsong said. "What do you do?"

"I've got a band," I said without thinking—and then I remembered the vocalists we were touring with. "And I *sing.*"

"Where're you playing?"

"The Steel Pier, in Atlantic City. We do rock and roll to a big-band beat. That's our thing."

"I'll come down there and take a listen," Jim said. "Let's see what you've got." Jim brought back a glowing report to Epic, and it was agreed we would come to New York to make some instrumentals. I well remember our first get-together in the city, because Jim took me to lunch at a Chinese restaurant, which was a little finer than anything I had previously encountered. I ordered a hamburger. We had a good laugh over my small-town ways, and became good friends as much for the honesty between us as the fact that we respected each other's musical talents.

Our first album was based on the theme "a young man with a band." It was a combination of big-band sound and rock and roll—the first of its kind. It received a lot of air play because stations could use most of the pieces as background music, and the disc jockeys loved it. A second album, "Bobby Vinton Plays for His Li'l Darlin's," was an attempt to do the same thing, and though it was directed to teen-agers it lacked the vocals that were necessary for a hit.

My press clippings were getting longer. But about the time *Billboard* magazine voted me and the guys the most promising band of the year, Epic called to say they wanted to wind up my contract. I wasn't selling enough to make money for them. I decided to go to New York and hang around Epic's offices until I found out exactly what was happening.

One thing I discovered was that my contract called for two more sides. While I was waiting for a decision from their lawyers and A&R—artists' representatives—men on what they planned to do with me, I did a little snooping, as is my habit, on the desks in their outer offices. There was a pile of rejects—records sent in over the transom by hopeful artists—on one desk. I felt like a reject, too. I said, "Say hello to a friend—we're in this together." As I looked through the stack, I spotted an interesting title, "Roses Are Red." Out of all the songs there I decided to play this one. As soon as I heard it, I said to myself, "I'm not really a singer, but this sounds to me like a song that could go over." I thought I could sell enough records with that song to get us out of a deficit and have the chance to make another band album.

The attorneys walked back in and told me they would give me another try—on a single. Jim Fogelsong said he felt he had done all he could with me as a bandleader, but perhaps there was someone else in the Columbia organization who was more in tune with my kind of music. "We'll record you as a vocalist, and we'll give you someone more your own age." He introduced me to Bob Morgan as my new producer.

Morgan immediately asked if I had any songs in mind. "There's one I wrote in the army," I said, "It's called 'Mr. Lonely'—and there's one on this reject pile that I think might work: 'Roses Are Red.'"

We got right down to work. Everything at the time involved one gimmick or another. A quartet was chanting "Shaboom, shaboom." So we tried a variety of rock and roll tricks with "Roses Are Red." The next day we listened to it, and it was terrible.

Always a rebel, I thought back to what made me stand out in school, in a band, in the army. It suddenly occurred to me that maybe the best gimmick of all was no gimmick. Wouldn't it stand out among all the noise of the day if we played it just as it was. What would happen if we sang it plain and straight and simple?

Six
Roses Are Red, Velvet Is Blue

We recorded four songs that day in New York. We did "Mr. Lonely" in a single take, and "Roses Are Red," plain and straight and simple, in two or three. When we were through with "Miss America" we began to get excited, and with the last one, "You and I," we thought we had a smash hit on our hands. Which ones should we put on my single, my last two sides of my Epic contract? The record would be released just before summer, so out of the three possibilities we chose "Roses Are Red" to back up "You and I" because of graduation time. In the lyrics of "Roses" there was an obvious reference to writing little verses like that in the yearbooks that were autographed at graduation. "Mr. Lonely" and "Miss America" would have to wait their turn.

The first people I took my record to for an opinion were, of course, my father, mother, Dolly, and my one-legged Polish gambler, Joe Gorlack. I knew I could communicate on the same level with them, and I knew they felt as I did about the record business. I played "You and I" for Joe, waited for a reaction, and then spun "Roses." The telltale tear came into his eye.

"Look, Bob," he said, "that gets to me."

I was surprised about his preference. "Are you putting me on?" I asked.

"I'm telling you if it gets to me it'll get to everybody. You can bet on it." That's all I needed. From that moment on, I began to look for news about "Roses," and I decided to promote it myself, if necessary.

At first it looked as if Joe had been mistaken. The promotion men at Epic, Sol Rabinowitz and Len Levy, said that there was some reaction to "You and I" from California, but there was no word about "Roses." Sol said "Roses" had been played for two weeks by WBZ in Boston, and then was taken off the play list when no one responded. Well, I thought, I'm a new artist and the Epic label is still relatively unknown. Maybe the trouble is that my record company doesn't believe in me. I had one last way to make them believers. I'd show them what "Roses" could do with a little promotion behind it.

I had three things going for me: the faith of Joe Gorlack, my experience in promoting my own Melody label in the Pittsburgh area, and the help of a man named Solly Solomon. I had met Solly a few years before in the coffee shop of the Carlton House in Pittsburgh. When I was pushing my own label, I used the pay phone and a seat at the counter there as my office. An extemporaneous office like that had, of course, several disadvantages. Once a perplexed voice said, "Is this the Bobby Vinton office? We've been trying to reach you all day but some coffee shop keeps answering." But the chief advantage of my coffee-shop office was that it was cheap and allowed me to meet people like Solly. He was the public relations man for Columbia Records in the Pittsburgh area. We hit it off, and he told me, "If you ever get with Columbia, I'll do a job for you." As fate would have it, I wasn't with Columbia, but with the next best thing, their subsidiary. It was time to pull out all the stops.

At the distributor's warehouse in Pittsburgh, about a thousand copies of "Roses" were gathering dust in a corner. I got together all the money I had and bought them. Then I packed them into the same little red Plymouth I had used as my delivery truck for Melody Records, and took off around the tristate area. Slowly but surely I made the rounds of each National Record Mart and every other record store in that corner of western Pennsylvania, Ohio, and West Virginia and tried to distribute twenty-five to each. I was willing to *give* them away, but it's not always that easy. One store owner would complain about fouling up his bookkeeping. Another would ask if "Roses Are Red" was a kids' song. But I had been through all this before, and eventually got more than nine hundred records in the stores.

Of all the stores I visited, I never have forgotten the time I tried to sell three teen-agers in the presence of a skeptical manager. He didn't want to handle my records at any price, so I told him, "Watch how this song sells," as three typical girls came in the store. "My name is Bobby Vinton," I said to them, "and I'd like you to hear my newest recording, 'Roses Are Red.'" When the song was finished, I asked for their reaction.

"It's terrific, I love it!" said one. Another chimed in, "It's going to be a hit!"

"Would you like to buy one!" I asked confidently.

"Oh, no!" And they put the record back on the counter.

"But you said you liked it so much," I argued. "I'll even sign it for you."

"We only buy records when they're hits on the radio," one answered.

"Look, I'm right here!" I protested. "You said it's going to be a hit."

They turned to walk away. "We'll buy it when it's a hit and when all our friends have it, too." And that's the story of the teen-age market to this day.

But after several days of this, I finally had Pittsburgh, Wheeling, and Steubenville plastered with "Roses" records. Now I had to get the disc jockeys to play it. I had to prove to my own record company that if the records were in the stores and it got good air time it would sell. And I had an idea how to go about this, too.

I found a trusting florist who sold me dozens and dozens of red roses on account. By all standards, I was out of my mind. I had spent my last dollar on my own record and now I was going into hock for promotion materials. If it didn't work, I'd be cleaned out and would have to go looking for the type of job I supported myself with in school: selling home-study courses, gardening, working for the county assessor. The possibility that I would fail, however, really didn't occur to me. I blindly undertook the job of getting the d.j.'s to spin "Roses Are Red."

Although I had a lot of friends at the stations, like Clark Race, Art Pallan, and Chuck Brinkman, I knew I'd have to come up with a different approach to convince the other disc jockeys to pay attention to my record. My idea, my first promotion stunt, was to wrap a dozen red roses with the record and deliver them to each d.j. in the Pittsburgh area. Clark was a good friend and didn't have to be promoted; he was the first to play "Roses Are Red" in the area. But when I loaded up my car with roses and came to KDKA, I began to get second thoughts about walking in with a handful of roses "for the boys." It might look a little strange. I stood in front of the station trying to build up my courage, and almost forgot why I was there as a stunning young lady in a short skirt came down the street. She was my mystery lady.

Back in those days, short skirts weren't *in*. And she had beautiful legs if I had ever seen any. In an instant I realized that she could be my entree to the disc jockeys. I followed her down the street and introduced myself. She listened sympathetically as I told her the whole story of my record and my promotion idea. She gave me a look as if I were crazy, then smiled and said, "Why not?" And she rode around with me from one station to the next, having no trouble at all delivering the records buried in red roses.

Every d.j. played the song at least once that day.

Solly Solomon and I checked the record stores in a couple of days. "Roses Are Red" was sold out! And now I waited for the payoff—a call from my record company.

"You won't believe this!" they said excitedly. "We've got fantastic news for you. We've just sold almost a thousand records in the Pittsburgh area!"

I expressed astonishment. "Wow! That's terrific! I don't know how to thank you for breaking my record for me." Solly explained the roses promotion to them, which they immediately tried in the major cities of the country. At WBZ in Boston, "Roses" went back on the air and within two months had become one of the all-time best-selling singles in New England. Joe Gorlack was right; I had my first gold record. Even more surprising, "Roses" became an overnight hit all over the world and left me in a daze—but that's another story.

I have never forgotten that "mystery gal" who was so kind to me at a time in my life when I needed help from someone so badly. She expected nothing in return, but I always hoped to be able to pay her back in some way. Many years later, when I opened at the Riviera Hotel in Las Vegas, I thought I finally had an opportunity to do something nice for my long-legged friend. I asked Art Pallan at KDKA in Pittsburgh to make an announcement on the air about the whole story and to ask her to come forward. I invited her and her family to come as my guests to my opening at the Riviera. But she couldn't be found.

Somewhere, sometime, I know I will find her.

Perhaps it will be through the story I have told here. I want her to know that, though we little suspect it at the time, it's the little, simple things in life that people do for each other that turn out to be so big as the years go by.

SEVEN
If Only There Was
Time to Enjoy It . . . .

As our plane settled down over Cologne, Germany, I saw the spires of the famous cathedral that had survived the leveling bombing of the city in the Second World War. Twenty years earlier, I might have been coming in as a bombardier. But now I was arriving to record a love song.

I stepped off the plane, I walked to the fenced area around the airport terminal, I saw the banners and heard the screams of a crowd of young people. It was all a dream. I was receiving a bigger welcome by far in this city so strange to me than I had received in my hometown. And the events of the next few months would be so crowded that they would be only a blur for the rest of my life. I have often wanted to go back and relive those days now that I have time to enjoy them. The things that were so hazy for me then I can see so much clearer now.

It was a thrill enough to know that "Roses Are Red" was number one in a country like Germany; it was even more devastating to hear it, in English, on the German radio stations. And now they wanted it recorded in the German language. So here were Bob Morgan and I, at the Columbia studios in Cologne, making a record in a foreign language of a song that had come off a reject pile several months before. But as soon as my recording session was over, I boarded a plane back to Fort Dix—and the army.

In the reserve program I was in, everyone had to put in two weeks of active duty a year for five years. Because of my trip to Germany, I wasn't able to put in my time with my regular unit, so I had received permission to delay my stint until the following two weeks. As might have been expected, this slight switch resulted in the loss of all my papers, so that when I showed up for duty no one expected me or would let me in. I insisted that my papers would arrive, and meantime I would put in my time so as to keep my schedule intact.

Day after day went by without any word from the army, but my superiors held their breath and accepted my presence. Then Bob Morgan called from New York: they were having trouble with some of my new arrangements, and would like me to get a weekend pass.

"Impossible, Bob," I reported; "I'm not even officially here. But there must be a piano somewhere on

77

the base. Come on down and we'll find a few keys."

He agreed, and I waited patiently all day Saturday for his visit. Morgan is a Clark Gable type, who could talk himself into Sing Sing. I told him we could find a piano in the basement of the chapel. We crept down to the chapel, forced a basement door, and by flashlight started going over the keys in question on an old upright. He was scribbling notes and I was sounding chords and "ta-ta-taing" along.

All of a sudden the room lit up like a television studio and a dozen MP's stood around us. Morgan was dressed in the boating clothes he had been wearing that afternoon, and I was graced by my GI pajamas. "What's the meaning of this, gents?" a captain yelled.

"We're finding keys," I said lamely.

"Let's see your papers—who are you guys?"

Morgan offered his wallet, thus proving he was an intruder, and I gave a pained look as I remembered I had no papers at all. "We can explain everything," Morgan said, as they led us off to the guardhouse.

Army experiences tend to merge together, and in my case especially so because I have always seemed to have a fondness for costumes and uniforms. Part of this has to do with being an entertainer. But even as a child I enjoyed being a make-believe soldier, just as later I wouldn't feel uncomfortable in the role of a prince. Another episode stands out in my mind from my *real* army days.

I was back at Fort Dix for my annual two weeks of active duty. This time I was Stanley Vinton, the way my dog tags read, my real name. Occasionally a soldier would approach me and inquire, "Aren't you Bobby Vinton?" and I'd discover a different side of the appeal of the popular singer. I had thought all my fans were girls, and only secondarily their boyfriends; now I realized men liked to identify with me, and when there were no women around and therefore no competition they were quite sympathetic to me. And then it was just like the old days with my band and in college: there was a Sergeant Bilko in every barracks and a Private Hargrove doing KP. I must have said hello by phone to every guy's girlfriend.

After a few days on the base I got a telegram from Epic Records: I had to make a few recordings in New York within the next week, or miss the opportunity to get some new songs in my upcoming album. It wasn't life-and-death, but an opportunity. I had to get a one-day pass, and it could only come from the so-called toughest sergeant in the army, who couldn't care less about a singer.

As I stood outside his office I heard him roar, "I don't care who he is or what he needs . . . send this Vinton in!"

The door closed behind me. "Well, Vinton, what is it?" he shouted for the benefit of his audience outside. "Get over here!"

"So?"

"I need a day, just a day, in New York. I have to record some songs," I said, taking the direct approach.

"So you want a pass, do you?" The crowd could hear that one.

"Yes, sir."

He leaned across the desk and whispered in as sweet a voice as I've ever heard, "Look, Vinton, I'm a singer, too. Listen: When I-rish eyes are smiling . . . ."

I stopped him and smiled, not just because I knew I was on my way to New York but because he had a great voice. "Sergeant, I'm not kidding, that's not bad."

"Naw . . ."

"This is what I mean. You're no teen-ager, and you're not going to the Met, but you've probably heard the singing policeman on the 'Ed Sullivan Show . . .'"

"Yeah—you mean—"

"I mean you may have a great novelty act. You've got a voice."

"Are you willing to have a test?"

"Where? You mean go to New York?"

"Sure! We can go together. I'll introduce you to the guys at the studio and we'll cut a demo. What've you got to lose?—it's just a few bucks."

"I'll let you know. Now, listen, Vinton—not a word of this to anyone."

"No, *sir*."

As I saluted and turned to the door, he bellowed, "That's all, Vinton!"

Two days later the sergeant took me aside and explained that his wife objected. It wasn't the money, he said, but he was going to make a fool of himself—if not at the studio, at least to the men. I reassured him. "The pass isn't that important to me. I really mean I

The sailor boy with two proud parents to give him confidence.

My father was nicknamed "Showboat" because he always had a flashy car in his single days. He kept the nickname when I took the place of the car.

Grandma "Ba" was a strong influence on me as a child. Blanche and Kasper, my mother's parents, had an old-country atmosphere in the home just down the street—and a piano.

My first communion picture recorded my first real grown-up suit.

My musical career dates back to the time I first held my father's saxophone —at the age of four.

By age 16 I had formed my own "kids' band" with the help of my father's bandstands —note the "SV."

Then it was graduation and off to college.

Before long, my father and I joined forces, and we became the "Bob Vinton" band. My mother graced our official photo as our female vocalist. Chuck Cochran is at the piano, Joe Dybell is behind me at my right, my father is directly to my right.

During college I joined with a comedian and singer to form a nightclub act known as the Hi-Lites.

But the army ended that brief career. I didn't think of it at the time, but we always remained a close family. That was the real trio.

Our first recording contract with Epic gave our band something to cheer about as we toured the tri-state area of Ohio, Western Pennsylvania, and West Virginia.

The "young man with a band"—my first promotion picture for a recording company.

Ed Sullivan, who gave me good TV exposure in my early days, always introduced me as "The young Bobby Vinton." We hit it off from the very start, even though I had a reputation at the time of being the bad boy of TV.

The place for entertainers to break in
was New York's Copacabana. I appeared there for seven straight years
and set the attendance record for a
single day when I did three standing-
room-only shows. This was the entertainer's showcase, and here Sophie
Tucker gave me the finest compliment
—one of her irrepressible laughs.

My first promotion pic under the direction of a show biz genius, Allen
Klein. Al had a knack for finding the
right public for each entertainer.

Cutting our first record under my own label—"Melody." (Funny how that word keeps coming back!) With me, left to right, buddies Jim Drake, Bob McCoy, Sammy Lombardo.

Al Klein debates the issues at our infamous "lockout" in the Hullabaloo debacle, where I earned the reputation of being a trouble-maker for things everybody else was trying to do for me.

I played the son of Maureen O'Hara and John Wayne in the movie *Big Jake.* After my "death scene," Duke gave me a fatherly look he didn't reserve for the cameras.

Life magazine ran a ten-page feature on me in 1965 with the theme, "Who's Bobby Vinton?" Al Klein couldn't resist this headline at the crossroads of the world, Times Square, for my record-breaking appearance at the Copacabana. (*Irving Newman*)

Football started for me in grammar school and has carried over into life with my kids. Hank Stram, then coach of the powerful Kansas City Chiefs, was my Polish football mentor.

LEFT: I came to know Elvis Presley in Las Vegas. Here Pete Bennet, my press agent, tries to soak up the aura of Colonel Parker, Elvis's super flak.

ABOVE RIGHT: I've always believed to be a crowd-pleaser you've got to project your emotions personally to your crowd. They told me not to try to woo the women in South America, but here I am in Caracas.

BELOW RIGHT: When "Melody of Love" swept the country, I had no idea it would become much larger than a song. People like that great human being Mayor Daley took it to heart— not only politically, but socially for what it meant to "ethnic power" of all kinds. *(Chicago Tribune Photo)*

"Polish Power" was flashed across Times Square as the major cities of the country took the lyrics of a song seriously for the first time.

ABOVE RIGHT: A Bobby Vinton show is a handclapping, foot-stomping performance—for kids of all ages. On the county fairgrounds or in the spotlight at the Palmer House, I aim to please.

BELOW RIGHT: My drummer/leader Lloyd Morales and I have been traveling the country for seven years, from Hawaii to Puerto Rico. A few key people travel with me to every performance, and we put together the rest of our big band sound from local musicians. *(Mun Wong)*

Ted Knight *is* Polish and Phyllis Diller could be anything—but they both came to have fun on the Polish Prince's three-ring circus.

In my case, I think the traveling of show business has helped our marriage. Dolly says every home-coming is a honeymoon. At least I know I have to try harder to be a good parent—and trying harder, isn't that the story of my life?

After the loss of my father, Vince Carbone filled a great void in my life as my personal manager and jack-of-all-trades in arranging my appearances. Vinnie was a saxophonist in the original Glen Miller Orchestra.

The Polish Prince

My home

think you have a chance. Take it now, or you'll always regret it."

I have seen many talented guys whose wives took every opportunity to scuttle them. It was probably jealousy—the fear that the husband would break into something and go on to a new career, leaving her behind. Or the fear of making a mistake. Some men love and lose, some never love, and some never even *try* to love.

Unfortunately, the "singing sergeant" didn't take the chance.

In this whirlwind period after the dizzying success of "Roses Are Red," I had many opportunities to enjoy that feeling of having tried—and *succeeded*. I was doing scattered shows, and all of a sudden found myself booked into the Fox Theater in Brooklyn as the headliner. Everything had come so fast: less than a year earlier I was playing with my band at the Paramount across the street, where the vocalists were the stars and we were just doing backup. Some of the headliners had complained about me to the manager because I was upstaging them. Even though I was only the bandleader, I was winning the audience over. The manager of the theater called me in and asked me to stick to playing the saxophone.

"I hate to tell you this, kid," he said. "You're a nice guy, but I've had some complaints from the singers that you are stealing the show. They want you to stop singing. You were hired to play the sax and warm up the audience with some instrumental numbers, and that's *all*." I knew that, inside, he was sorry to have to tell me this. So in a joking way I told him that someday I'd be a big singing star and I'd boycott the Paramount. Not only wouldn't I perform for him, but maybe I'd make a movie some day and I wouldn't let them show there.

He looked at that skinny kid and said, "You know, with that attitude, you just might make it! I'm going to let you continue singing. I've got a daughter who's starting to break into the movies, and I wouldn't like it if someone tried to hold her back. Her name is Suzanne."

"I wish her luck, Mr. Pleshette."

Today, I often see Mr. Pleshette at Matoe's Restaurante having dinner with his wife and daughter, Suzanne Pleshette.

When I returned to make good on my boast, the Paramount had been closed, but I had the next best thing in the Fox. But there was a problem. Rock and roll was in, and the headline performer had to follow all that excitement with his two best songs. My second big recording, "Rain, Rain Go Away," was just out, so I had to close with that and "Roses Are Red." On the opening show I felt I bombed. It became obvious to everyone that those two ballads just didn't have the excitement of the rock performers. I was at a loss about what to do. Fortunately, I was developing a fan club and my supporters were aware of my dilemma. One of them came to me after the opening show and suggested, simply, that I walk into the crowd and maybe kiss a couple of girls. It was a wild idea. We were in Brooklyn, not Forest Hills, and the kids were as rough as I remembered Dolly's neighbors were

82

back in Canonsburg. But I also remembered that time on New Year's Eve in my father's band when I got away with it. Nobody would have thought, at that time in the early sixties, of going out into an audience like that. And maybe that's why the idea appealed to me.

The shock of walking out into the aisles, as no entertainer had done before, protected me. It was an instant success and started me on a style that I have traded on ever since. I learned that day at the Fox, once and for all, that all kinds of people, old and young, go to a show as if they were going to a party. I like to be right out in the middle of it.

With the best-selling record in the world, everyone assumed I was a millionaire. But out of the proceeds from "Roses Are Red" had to come all the recording costs from my previous instrumental albums. And even though I would follow this success with one hit after another, just about a year later I would be renting an apartment in Los Angeles—for $125 a month.

EIGHT
Do Me a Favor—
Stop Playing My Song

One of the first rules of the entertainment or record business is to follow up on a hit with something else of the same kind. But how do you follow up the number one record in the world? Epic and I were discussing this question as "Roses Are Red" passed the one million mark and then two million. Eventually, it would sell more than three million singles.

My first choice was the song I had composed in the army and we had recorded among the first four vocals Bob Morgan and I had done for Epic. It hadn't been released, but it had great emotional meaning to me: "Mr. Lonely." It had passed the Joe Gorlack test. But my record company disagreed. They thought that "Roses" was successful because it appealed to a sing-along mentality, and among other records I had cut for them was a similar thing, "Rain, Rain Go Away." It had a singsong simplicity Epic thought was my style. I wanted something quite different.

After I had a number of top hits to my credit, Epic seemed to feel I was some kind of a fluke. Clive Davis called a meeting of all the A&R men and demanded to know how that week I could be outselling all their other artists *combined*. "How can that be?" was his attitude: something must be wrong with the other guys, and not *right* with me. Billy Sherrill, my new record producer in Nashville, smiled when he told me this—as our record "I Love How You Love Me" hit the million and one-half mark. But I'm getting ahead of my story.

At this crucial stage in my life as a vocalist, Epic couldn't decide how to follow up my first hit. They wanted time to think about it. I was trying to develop myself as a live performer, and it was more difficult in those days when the teen-age idols were considered to be some kind of freak. None of them were thought to have lasting talent. Screaming teen-agers were thought to be a cult. Their stars were talented only in making a hit record every now and then. So my popular record success did little to get me good club dates or television appearances. I've had to build a following little by little, year after year, gradually proving myself to my buyers and my audience. While "Roses" was rising in the charts, I was driving through the Midwest from one small club to another, wondering why the media had such an anti-youth orientation. Today it's just the opposite.

I turned on the radio one day and heard an awfully familiar tune. It was "Mr. Lonely," only it was being sung not by me but by Buddy Greco. I stopped the car and ran to the nearest phone. Levy and Morgan at Epic told me the sad truth: they had decided to give my song to Greco, whom they were grooming as their next superstar. "Rain, Rain Go Away" had already been released.

Little by little I began to get the story from them. Their bottom-line decision was that I was really a songwriter—after all, I had written "Mr. Lonely"! The implication was that "Roses" was a one-shot performance. A flood of self-doubt swept over me. I remembered what disc jockey Bob Tracy had told me in Pittsburgh—and I thought he knew me through and through: "You're a hustler—get a good girl singer. You play the sax, make records, and promote the band. I'm telling you this as a friend." And I remembered another friend, Chuck Daugherty, at WIP in Philadelphia. When he was in Wheeling at WKWK I used to take my Melody records down to him for his opinion. He saw my drive and enthusiasm, but he told me, "You'll never make it as a singer—why not sell time for my station?" When I told him I didn't have a car on a regular basis, he offered to drive me to and from Canonsburg. And I remembered how I was on the verge of being convinced that's what I should do. My best friends, who loved me and believed in me, were saying, "You'll do something, but singing isn't it!" And now even Epic was saying, "You're a musician and arranger, not a singer. That's how you came to us."

I decided to fight it out. I had to prove I was a singer with a record I didn't choose, "Rain." I had to overcome a competing artist with my own company, singing my own song. And all of a sudden, I discovered I had a new fight on my hands, which went back to my first meeting with Epic. When disc jockey Dick Lawrence had taken me to New York and sold my tape to Epic, the song I recorded was "I Love You the Way You Are." I had forgotten that this was given back to Lawrence, and he now owned it. It was a far better song than "Rain," and in fact even today a song with similar lyrics has become a hit: "I Love You Just the Way You Are." (The writer of this song, Billy Joel, I like to think, listened to it on the radio as a youth and was subconsciously influenced by it!) In any case, Dick Lawrence, never one to be left at the starting gate, was well aware of the success of "Roses Are Red" and was prepared to have a little follow-up of his own to that hit. He took his tape to a small label, Diamond, and released it. Before you could say "Epic," his song—*my* song—was climbing the charts.

When "Rain" at last came out, it was up against that formidable obstacle. Worst of all, "I Love You the Way You Are" was strongly entrenched in the two big markets of the country, Chicago and New York. People asked me, "What do you care—aren't you getting royalties from it?" I might get some, but it was a mixed-up business and you couldn't always depend on an accurate report of sales. Besides, the object of the record business is to hit one out of the park; I don't play baseball to draw walks. I had to find a way to promote "Rain," but they weren't playing it in the top two markets of the country. In order for "Rain" to be number one in the country, all the major markets must be playing it. I then had to try to get the two biggest disc jockeys in America *not* to play my record.

I got on the phone to Chicago's top d.j. at the time, Dick Biondi at WLS. "Dick, I'd like to ask you a favor. Will you please stop playing 'I Love You the Way You Are'?"

"You've got to be kidding!"

"Do it as a favor," I pleaded.

"You know I can't do that. It's been number one in Chicago for five weeks. I'm going to keep on playing it, and that's that."

Deep down inside, I knew that "Rain" wasn't number one material. But I gave it a try also in New York. I called Murray "the K" Kaufman at WINS. He gave me the same answer. There was nothing any d.j., Epic, or I could do. My follow-up record could never overtake its cousin, and my big chance to capitalize on my success with "Roses" was nipped in the bud.

But it wasn't the end of the story for "Mr. Lonely." I had always kept in close touch with the d.j.'s in the major cities. They were aware that Buddy Greco was singing a song I had written and I had hoped to release myself. So they were sympathetic to my cause and, I think, soft-pedaled the Greco version. In spite of Epic's high hopes for it, it gradually died. At least I had that satisfaction.

Years pass. After eleven consecutive hits, my company decides to release an album of Bobby Vinton's greatest hits. But there's a twelfth track to fill. Epic asks me what I want for that spot. I say, "'Mr. Lonely' may not have been a hit to anybody else, but it was to me." So it finally appears in an album, and the d.j.'s begin to play it from the album, especially those who remember the Buddy Greco incident. The demand starts growing for a release of "Mr. Lonely" as a single. I'm in Los Angeles at the time it finally comes out as a single. Only now no one wants to play it. One reason the newer disc jockeys give is that is has all kinds of high, falsetto notes. And, they say, it bombed once with Buddy Greco—why is it all that different now? So I have to fight that record originally to keep it from succeeding, and in the end I have to fight it as a failure. I go to the distributor in Los Angeles with a proposition. "Look, do you want to make some money? Bet all these guys it's going to be number one all over the country! I'll take all bets."

The rest of the story you can guess. When he saw the confidence I had in my record, he got behind it with enthusiasm of his own. And throughout all the years since then, a night doesn't go by at one of my shows without a request for the song I wrote in Fort Dix.

It became one of the biggest records with servicemen stationed around the world.

Nine
Thank You,
St. Espanola,
Wherever You Are

I don't like to parade my personal life in front of my public. I don't bring family or religion or politics onto the stage, as, for reasons of their own, many of my colleagues choose to do. But if you ask me about any of these things, I won't hide my feelings. Recently I was standing on the front steps of my local church talking with the pastor about something *I* should know about—attendance. The kids seem to be missing the act on Sunday mornings. And those who do attend seem to be looking around for everything but the main attraction. While talking to our priest, I expressed my feelings and opinions on the subject.

"Kids are smarter today than when we were kids. After all, I've been raising five of my own and have some firsthand experience. Kids today see more of the world—through television and the rest of the mass media. Before they learn to read or write, they can spot a dumb commercial."

The pastor nodded. "The Church has tried to keep pace. We've got folk Masses, more up-to-date music—"

"Yes, but I think that's going the wrong way," I said. Styles in music change. But a choir and organ music will always be inspiring, bringing us closer to someone greater than ourselves. Instead of trying to make the music more modern, why not make the presentation of the *message* more up to date?

"What do you propose?" I was asked.

My answer was that the Church has to compete in the techniques of modern media. The Church is one of the most powerful organizations in the world. Why can't it do what our politicians do? Use the best writers, psychologists or experts available to come up with one sermon each week that would get its point across. Send out to every church the best-thought-out message these people can come up with. Make it a powerful sermon that will work all over the country. It doesn't have to replace the sermon completely—let each priest or minister give his personal touch to the message. But have something every Sunday that competes for the attention of the kids—not to mention the adults. Recently I heard a visiting missionary at my church give a sermon and I was very moved. He had been using it for years to get his point across. And he used it because it worked. Perhaps a church board could select the very best lecturers available. A lot of changes have occurred in the Church in recent years; this is one that I think could really mean something.

I was warming to my subject. I told my pastor that I thought the services are too long to hold our attention nowadays. I remember how our parish priest in Canonsburg could sense when he was making it uncomfortable for everyone, so he limited the Mass to a half hour. The Szelong express, we called it. It was always packed on Sunday. And why not have Mass on television on every Sunday morning instead of just Christmas and Easter? It can't substitute for personal attendance, but with good music and a strong sermon it would be a whole lot better than what's on the tube now. And this should apply to any church or synagogue. Television, I'm convinced, is too strong a medium not to use, or to use half-heartedly. If you have a good coach, use him! Isn't that what St. Paul was trying to do when he wrote all those letters to his friends in various churches?

I'm not a preacher, but religion has touched my life many times and I'm convinced it's one of the strongest social forces we have. We'd need a policeman on every corner without it.

Walking up Fifth Avenue, I found myself in front of the biggest cathedral I had ever seen in my life. I knew it must be St. Patrick's. I had recorded "Roses" in another church, down on East Thirtieth, a big red-brick building the studios had taken over because it had perfect acoustics. Johnny Mathis, Tony Bennett, and dozens of other stars had made some of their biggest hits there. I thought it would be a nice touch to wind up my New York stay by visiting another famous church.

Inside, the long shadows of the afternoon cast a

medieval spell over the stillness of the cavernous structure. Around the sides of the cathedral were numerous alcoves and side altars, each with a handful of people praying or lighting candles before it. As I moved across the marble floors in awe, I searched for a spot where I might rest for a moment, to take in the splendor of the scene, which was for me a part of the rich European heritage of the Church I had been raised in. I came to a spot where the candles weren't lit, a niche where a small pedestal supported a statue of what I dimly read as "St. Espanola." Here's a saint who's just like me, I thought—*unnoticed*.

On an impulse, I dropped a few coins in the box, took a match, and lit three candles. I looked up and said "St. Espanola, I've just released a record called 'Roses are Red'. I need a miracle. I don't know if I'm a good singer. The song is very simple, but with your help it could be a hit."

That was my prayer, whether it was articulate or not. You have already heard all the reasons why "Roses" eventually worked, so it might seem presumptuous of me to claim that St. Espanola had anything to do with it—on the other hand who's to say?

Later, after "Roses" was an assured success, I asked arranger Bob Mersey if he remembered the record sounding that good at the session. "I don't even remember it," he said honestly. Whatever part St. Espanola may have played, I didn't leave him out for the next five years of my recording life. Every time I recorded a song, I went back to him and lit a candle. And I had one big hit after another. But you can't keep going back to friends for favors, so I stopped asking for hit records. I had sold millions and I felt enough was enough. Even when my record popularity started to fade, I didn't go back to see him. My home was in California. My popularity on the turntable ebbed.

As we will see, I needed all the help I could get some years later with that other big record that would rejuvenate my life, "My Melody of Love." When the fate of that record was hanging in the balance, I found myself once again in New York, for an appearance at the Waldorf Astoria. Walking down Fifth Avenue, I came to St. Patrick's and decided to visit my saint in the corner. I said, "I know you're not Polish, and I said I wouldn't be back for another favor, but I really need help with a Polish song. This is the last miracle I'll ask you for."

I don't know whether you believe in miracles or not. I don't really know if I believe in them. But that's the way it happened. There are prayers of thanksgiving, too. And with my Polish song I had more to be thankful for than ever. So after the success of that record I went back to the cathedral. I approached the familiar niche, but there was nothing in sight. Surely I didn't have the wrong spot! I saw some workmen replacing pads on the kneelers in the pews nearby. "Where's the statue that used to be here?" I asked. They shrugged their shoulders. "St. Espanola, the one right behind the candles."

"There's never been a statue there," one man said.

"St. Espanola?" another volunteered. "I've never heard of that name." They gave me a quick look, and went back to their work.

The statue was gone but I left my prayers of thanks at the altar. Whenever I think of St. Espanola it's always with a prayer of thanksgiving.

TEN
Girls Always Look Best in Church

Since I was now traveling all over the country, with an occasional trip overseas, I had to make up explanations for my friends about why I was seeing a girl from my hometown. "She's just my Canonsburg girl friend," I told them. Dolly Dobbin was still in high school, and when I was home I usually had to go to a performance date on weekends. Our time together was accordingly limited. Our best chance to get together was Tuesday nights after my National Guard duty, when she would have french fries and other treats ready for me and her parents would allow me to stay till midnight.

I liked the way she looked in church. Wherever I went there were show girls and squealing fans, there were sophisticated ladies and red-hot mamas, but to me there was nothing prettier than a young woman dressed up for church. My advice to young men on the lookout for a date is to start here. In their freshness and finery, the girls of Canonsburg had an indefinable beauty; and Dolly was the belle of the vestibule.

With my busy schedule during this period of my life—the hectic running around to performances and promotions—being in church also cleared my head. I've always found my mind wandering in many directions in that atmosphere, with just enough distractions to cause me to ask myself the right questions. It was my form of psychotherapy. And that busy schedule didn't give us much time for regular dating. So we compromised. I would take her with me on the one-day shows or promotions I had within driving distance of Canonsburg, just as other people on dates would take a long drive in the country. That would kill two birds with one stone. "You're either the dumbest or the smartest girl I've ever known," I told her.

One of our frequent trips to the surrounding area involved a record hop—an institution no longer in existence because it, too, was branded as a form of payola. A disc jockey would arrange a hop at a dance hall that could accommodate perhaps a thousand people. He would inform the record company that this was a command performance for one of their stars, or he would simply say, "Who do you have? I'll play his records all week if he'll appear at my dance." Kids would be admitted for a nominal amount. And the performer would autograph his records and photographs, and pretend to sing his latest hit while it was played over the loudspeakers. Everybody came out okay, nobody got hurt, and best of all, the kids had a place to go. You would think that every legislator in the country would be in favor of this happy result, but no. It was payola, and it had to go. The amount of money that changed hands was like a five-cent tip compared to what goes on in any election campaign. And like every other sanctimonious search for ethics, the campaign against payola made things infinitely worse. As we have seen, radio stations are now afraid to play anything but what appears on their "play list." Some three hundred new records are released each week, but only two or three are added to the tight list. So new talent has nowhere to go, kids are left with no choice but TV or the streets, and the whole nation is subjected to the sameness of a top twenty. That's how our government has managed to bring corruption to a halt.

Excuse the digression, but we *did* have fun, all of us, at record hops. The featured singer, of course, would maintain the pretense of being not only single but unattached. So when I brought Dolly along I would introduce her as my sister. Guys would come up and ask me if I could fix them up with her. "Sure," I'd say; "Dolly, I'd like you to meet . . . ." Equally, the girls would ask Dolly a lot of personal questions about me: "What's his favorite food? Does he sing around the house?" Just once this pleasant game almost came to a disastrous conclusion.

It was in East Liverpool, Ohio, in a desolate location way out in the country. We soon realized that these weren't the usual teen-agers. It looked as if we were the only ones who came in a car and who weren't wearing leather jackets. This evening was going to be a little bit different. Everyone was "feeling good," especially the girls, who seemed to have forgotten all about shyness and their boyfriends by the second number. And for their part, the guys began to take as much an interest in me as the girls—but for a different reason. Whatever the sudden interest, I knew it wasn't going to be healthy for me. I stopped the show right then and yelled, "Hey, I want to make an announcement. I want you to meet my girl friend, my only love, the only woman in my life, Dolly Dobbin!" The tension eased immediately and everyone had a great time.

It's somewhat ironic that this was the first crowd ever to hear a formal declaration of my relationship with Dolly. Off and on, I had been thinking about our future, but I didn't come to any conclusion until I was halfway around the world from her. One of my biggest engagements up to that time was a quick tour of New Zealand. As soon as I got off the plane, I was struck by the enthusiasm of the crowds. They gave me that sense of excitement that the Beatles received on their first trip to the United States. I was from a town called Canonsburg, and it had an aura to them as strong as the aura of Liverpool was to the Americans. Again, the importance of being *imported* overrode everything else.

I dislike staying at hotels, with their big lobbies, formal elevators, and stuffy rooms. I was fortunate in being able to rent a house for my short stay, with another entertainer, Gene Pitney, whose hit record at the time was "Town Without Pity." The house was a

99

beautiful old mansion in the country, but we were the only guests and it soon struck me that there was something strange about the place. There was a howling at night that couldn't be explained by wind. I began thinking of all the Frankenstein movies I had seen. And this experience of being in what I thought was a haunted house, in a strange country so far from home, drove all other thoughts out of my mind except the basics. I had thought that the wider I traveled, the more I would discover, but I learned this didn't apply to love. I was a wide-eyed kid with dreams of meeting all the beautiful women in the world. I was ready for excitement, romance. I had heard it in songs and had seen it in movies. I thought it was all "out there" to be discovered. I didn't know that what I really wanted all the while was right around me.

When my last show was over, I phoned Dolly and said, "We're getting married next week. If it's okay with you, have everything set up by the time I get back."

"Okay," she answered.

I wanted to tell my mother the news myself, so I told Dolly not to call her. But I couldn't get a call through. Well, I thought, I have to play Pittsburgh on the weekend, so the first chance for the wedding is the next Monday. I'll tell my mother in person when I get home. Little did I know that Father Szelong would act so swiftly. According to standard Church practice, the banns of marriage—announcements—have to be made in church three times before the wedding. Father Szelong agreed to make all three announcements on a single Sunday, a week before I got home. And my

100

mother was the last one to hear the news, when she heard it read from the pulpit that day.

Quite naturally she was upset by a wedding that was to occur on a Monday, with such haste, without anyone telling her. And a mother of an only child, from an Eastern European background, is especially protective of that child. When we sat down to talk about it, she asked me to think about my career. She couldn't understand why I wanted to tie myself down to a wife at just the time when my future was beginning to open up for me. "There's plenty of time. You're too young," she pleaded. "You've got big things ahead of you."

I told my mother that Dolly was the girl I was going to marry, if it was this year, next year, or the year after that. I realized that I wanted to have two lives: a private life with a home and family, and at the same time a public life, pursuing the show-business career my mother knew was waiting for me. That's the way it has remained.

Dolly wanted to be married in church, with a traditional gown and everything that goes with it. But she wanted a home and family, not to be the wife of a superstar. That was her career—to be herself. And that has been our children's career. Their father is Daddy, not Bobby.

It was a Monday, a nuptial High Mass at St. Genevie, the Polish church where we had gone to school for eight years, with only close family and friends attending. And on that day, I fainted three times. I could hear my Polish grandmother crying in the background. As Dolly and I knelt side by side on a prie-dieu before the altar, I keeled over. My best man, my Polish friend Joe Dybell, carried me to the sacristy. I soon recovered myself and returned to the altar; everything seemed fine. It wasn't hot in church—this was just before Christmas. Dolly looked at me and asked, "Are you all right?" I turned white as I answered "Yes," and again keeled over backwards. I began to think the saints were trying to tell me something. But I still felt weak as I knelt again before the altar. I got to my feet and passed out on the way to the sacristy. This time Father Szelong turned to Dolly and said, "Look, you've already exchanged your vows. When Bob comes back, just get up and go. I'll finish the Mass later."

And so we did, and so he did.

ELEVEN
On the Road
from Canonsburg

On our honeymoon we set out on an odyssey that would take us to the high and low spots of the country, north and south, starting with a recording date in New York and ending with our arrival in Hollywood to knock on the door of movieland. It was Dolly's first trip outside the Pittsburgh area and the neighboring states. And although I had been all over the world and was launching a string of hit records, we still had to travel by car and we were still looking in store windows, saying, "I wish we could afford that."

From New York it was down to Nashville, to make a special album called "Hits of the Golden Groups." It was new country for both of us. But I had caught a cold driving down and was in no condition to give a decent performance, unless they were featuring "nasal" that year. I hadn't learned my lesson yet—that unless you give 100 percent you're only kidding yourself. I struggled through the album, trying to give an impersonation of myself as I might have sounded if well. Many years later I finally earned the rank to withdraw the album from the market. It's now a collector's item. The old adage is so true: there's always time to redo a rush job.

Even though Dolly had grown up with blacks in Canonsburg, she was unprepared for the South. One day she dropped me off at the studio and took our laundry down the street in a suitcase. The laundromat had two doors: "colored" and "white." She opened the suitcase and began carefully separating the clothes into two piles. She started the washer in the "white" room. When she took her colored clothes into the second room, a black woman said, "What are you doing here, honey?" Dolly answered, "These are my colored clothes." The woman laughed. "That means *people*, not clothes!"

And she began to experience along with me some of the hazards of being an entertainer. It wasn't all fan clubs and signing autographs. At a motel in Kentucky, we were asked if we were show-business people. Then we were asked to move on.

Even when we finally arrived in California, my traveling days were just beginning. I had hoped to capitalize on my reputation as a hit singer to land a movie part. But in the meantime I had to go back on the road, playing in small clubs and at colleges, to make a living. We settled into a small apartment, and waited, and traveled.

At last I got some good news from my agent. He

had something for me with a small but successful studio. Give me the details, I said.

"You're the male lead, the whole thing—and it's a new kind of picture," he bubbled.

"No kiddin'? What's it all about?"

"You're mobbed by girls in swimming suits—"

"Yeah, yeah—"

"You're the big guy on the beach. It's called *Surf Party*. And they don't want you to sing much—they want you to *act*."

"Hey, *great*." I didn't want to push, but I couldn't resist getting all the good news at once. "What's the deal? How much?"

"Six hundred."

"Six hundred *what*?"

"Six hundred dollars."

There was a long silence. I tried to wrap six hundred dollars around my mental calendar. "Alan Bregman," I finally said, "are you sure this is a movie? Movie stars live in big houses, they have yachts—"

"You're not a star, Bobby," and as a definite afterthought he continued, "yet."

"But six hundred dollars—I can't live for two weeks on that!"

"You have to start small in this business, Bobby. Then you make more later. By the way, it'll only take a week."

I must have been the lowest-paid leading man in the history of Hollywood. And Alan was right, it only took a week. That was probably the worst part of it.

I can't remember one detail of my brief life in

105

Hollywood. I try to put out of my mind everything that's incidental to my work. But I do remember the dangers and the embarrassments of being on the road alone, without advance men, managers, adequate sound systems, or the money to afford them.

And I learned to roll with the punches; you can never tell, I found out, when you're getting a blessing in disguise. Once I returned from a rehearsal to my motel, in Peoria, to find all my bags thrown in the hallway. In my room was a guy in a leather jacket, who informed me and my drummer, Lou Carto—who is as skinny as I am—that this was their annual motorcycle rally and their club had taken over the place. I looked at that gang and said, "No trouble at all. I'll just move over to some other motel in town. I'm Bobby Vinton. I'm doing a show in town. If you get a chance, stop by and I'll sing a song for you." I shrugged, gathered up my stuff, and found another motel.

In the club that evening I discovered that a group of local rowdies was living it up at the place. They were in the mood to cause trouble and were acting as if they had plans for me and my act. I didn't know how much longer I could keep the place in order, when all of a sudden the motorcycle gang appeared. I announced, "I'm dedicating my next song, 'Roses Are Red,' to my very special friends who have just arrived." You could hear a pin drop for the rest of the show.

It was on this tour that I learned what a handicap a performer had starting out without adequate sound systems or reliable musicians. At a college in North Carolina the orchestra was so bad I took my microphone down into the audience and sang without the orchestra. If they can't hear you, you can be Frank Sinatra and bomb every time. One of the biggest steps the new generation of rock groups has made is to take their own sound system with them—or to guarantee an equivalent system well in advance.

I remember arriving at a college in northern Montana about this time, on the afternoon of a concert I was to give, and being surprised to see no one around ready to practice. "What times does the band get here?" I inquired.

"What band?"

"My contract calls for a full band," I insisted. "Four saxophones, six brass, and so on."

"There aren't four saxophones within a hundred miles of here," the man said. "There's your accompaniment." He pointed to three guitarists on the stage.

At this point in my career, I felt I had to spend as little as possible of my fee for backup equipment and instrumentalists, so I thought I'd better do the most with what I was offered. I handed them some arrangements. "We don't read music," they said; "we'll follow you."

I thought: How do I get into jams like this? How could they possibly *follow* me and produce any kind of a show? Then I got a flash. "What do *you* play? May I hear something?" If they couldn't play my songs, I'd sing what they could play. As a matter of fact, they played their own material quite well, and we had a smash concert.

I was going through a new kind of basic training; I was learning to make the most of what I had to work with. Even in my shows today, I try to find out the strengths of the bands I'm given by the management and I gear my show to take advantage of those pluses.

Along the way, too, I discovered I had to control my desire to compete. I've always tried to win any contest I became involved in. It's a good old football philosophy: winning isn't everything, it's the only thing. But sometimes there are greater stakes than the immediate game. In these early touring days, when I had a couple of hit records on the way, I was invited to a poker game with a group of disc jockeys. It never crossed my mind that I was supposed to lose to them. I love poker, and I like to win. When the evening was over, I had cleaned them out. As we left the room, the local promotion man for my company said, "You fool! Don't you know those guys expected to pick up a little side money from us? If they don't like you, they'll never play your records." And as it turned out, I never did get much help from the d.j.'s in that city. I'm less naïve now.

During this period, 90 percent of my business was in the eastern United States. I was away from our little apartment for weeks at a time, and Dolly was expecting our first child. There was one last chance to make it in Hollywood. As Stan Kamen, my agent at William Morris, explained to me, the way you do it down here is to meet the right people. He told me that he had another young client with great potential, George Segal, and he was going to make both of us stars.

At last I got an invitation to have dinner with one of the important, right people, Danny Thomas. The long-awaited day arrived, and that evening Dolly gave birth to our first child Robbie, by a Caesarean section. As Dolly was wheeled into the recovery room, I thought how trivial "meeting the right people" was at a time like this. She had just gone through the longest day of her life. Then she gave me a knowing smile. "What I need is rest, Bob. Why don't you go?"

I met Danny that evening, and we became friends. I had the privilege of doing some of his famous St. Jude benefits for him. But that was all. I wasn't ready yet for the Hollywood game. But we were ready to go back to a place we could call home.

TWELVE
Bigger Than Life— and Without the Pictures

With a greater sense of permanence, we made a new home for ourselves in New York—first at Sutton Place and then in a sprawling house on Long Island. The mid-sixties were kind to my kind of music. It was at this time in my life that I met a man who would do more for me, and less for me, than any other person could have done. He was the greatest promoter in the business, but most of our promotions never seemed to get me anywhere. He had what can only be described as a *mind*, but he made some of the most mindless mistakes. He became my manager on a handshake and guided me through seven years of continuous growth, but I sometimes wonder if I didn't do more for him than he did for me. He was Allen Klein, a generous friend, the godfather to one of my children, and today a man at the very top of his field.

110

I think what this shrewd character did most for me was to impress me with myself. Before Allen stepped in, I didn't know I was Bobby Vinton. Allen didn't have a big name when we shook on our relationship; I got the unmistakable impression he was learning the business along with me. But he had the instinct to make me feel secure with myself and then to make me stand up to record companies, to promoters, and even to the biggest of all the media.

His underlying plan was to make me scarce. He knew I was the most-sought-after singer of the day. Each year brought another gold record. His idea was to increase the value of the gold by making me, the hottest vocalist going, an even scarcer commodity. In this period I made an appearance on "The Johnny Carson Show." Watching the show was one of the editors of *Life* magazine, who was taken aback when I was introduced as the number one record seller in the country. He decided to do a story on the "imposter"—a guy who claimed to be number one when nobody, he thought, had ever heard of him.

It happened that that was the year I received an award from *Billboard* magazine as the artist "most programmed" on the radio of all male singers. Frank Sinatra was second and Elvis Presley was third. Allen Klein told *Life* he didn't want that kind of "imposter" story. People believe what they read in the headlines, was his theory. But the more we refused to cooperate, the more pressure *Life* applied to get a story. The story grew from three pages, to five, to seven. When it finally ran as an eleven-page story, the writer had checked the facts with *Billboard,* and the headline

111

was changed to "The Most Famous Unknown." And I had the last laugh. I'm still around, and *Life* is a thing of the past.

I was to open a few weeks later at the Copacabana, the show-biz mecca in New York. Across town, Allen bought the biggest billboard in Times Square. Next to a large photo of me he ran the headline: "Bigger Than Life—Bobby Vinton." Playing three shows a night, I broke all attendance records for the Copa for a single evening. As far as I know, that record still stands.

Needless to say, Klein impressed on me the fact that *impressions* are important. In your private life you may want to be a "nice guy," but you've got to be professional about your career. Even to this day I've got to remind myself of this rule. When you work hard to reach the point where you receive top billing, you owe it to your audience as well as to yourself not to give it away. In a recent brochure announcing one of my performances, the name of my opening act was listed side by side with mine. It slipped by me, but I'm sure some of my fans caught it and might have wondered whether, if I was willing to take equal billing, I might not be putting on my best performance.

He had no fear of spending money to make the right impressions. When I opened at the Coconut Grove in Los Angeles, he made sure I'd be a hit. He hired one of the top PR firms in the country, Rogers and Cowen, and then almost bought the place out on his own, inviting as his guests every movie mogul and show-business executive he could think of. I think he had it in the back of his mind that he would get into the motion picture industry himself, in one way or another. Contrary to Allen's expectations, I learned you can't "buy" Hollywood. Rogers and Cowen had the contacts among the stars to guarantee that from twenty to fifty top names would be at my opening. When Allen checked to see how they were doing, they told him an unheard-of thing had happened: all fifty stars had turned them down. The only one who even heard of me was Dean Martin. And he knew me for a strange reason. The previous year I had been in the Health Club at the Sands in Las Vegas; I found myself next to Dean in the steam room. He came from my part of the country and was one guy I had always looked up to. I tried to impress him by telling him about my hit at the time, "Blue Velvet." "I've never heard of it," he said.

"But it's all over the radio—it's number one in *Billboard*."

"I never read *Billboard* if I don't have a record out," he replied.

"Well, *Billboard* has just awarded me the 'most programmed' male vocalist award. And Sinatra is second."

"Sinatra is second and you're first!"

"I'm only telling you what the d.j.'s said." Unknown to me, Frank Sinatra was lying next to Dean under a sheet. So a year later when Rogers and Cowen asked Martin to come to my opening, he told them, "Yeah, I know that smart-aleck kid. He's the guy who tried to tell me he was number one and Sinatra num-

113

ber two on the radio!" I was elated to find out that these two great singers had fumed over me as if I were competition!

That first experience with the Hollywood star system convinced me that parties and openings aren't my thing. I'm a non-goer to this day.

Allen had his sights set so high that he sometimes neglected the practical side of the business and caused his friends and clients much unnecessary grief. In my case, the grief began almost with my first transaction with him. In Los Angeles my first manager had been Alan Bregman. He had done a good job for me, but when I moved to New York it wasn't logical to continue with him. To terminate the contract, I would have to come up with about $20,000 due Bregman for his services. I asked Klein what to do about the legal entanglements, and my new manager gave me the first of one of his most characteristic lines: "Don't worry about it—trust me." He would resolve the whole problem.

A year went by without another word about the Bregman case. We moved from our furnished Manhattan apartment to a much larger home in Kingspoint, Long Island. Then the ax fell: Klein had swept the Bregman matter under the rug, and now I was presented by my lawyer Marty Machet with a judgment against me for almost four times the original amount, including legal fees and the rest. For the first and last time in my life, my bank accounts were closed. And shortly after we moved into our new house a moving van backed up to our front door and two burly men presented a court order to allow them to take all our possessions. Dolly and I broke out laughing. We had just moved from a furnished apartment and we had no furniture. We invited the men into an empty house, except for a playpen and a few chairs. "Take what you want," Dolly said.

It was quite a while before I dug myself out of that hole, and meanwhile Allen was innocently digging another one for me. Although he was representing singer Sam Cooke, I was still his hottest property, and he did everything he could to make me a superstar in the eyes of agents and buyers. In his enthusiasm he almost caused me to be blacklisted on my first big television appearance.

It happened in a New York studio where the hottest new variety show of the time was being taped. I was one of three or four headline singers or groups that were billed as the tops on either side of the Atlantic. Klein was keenly aware of the potential appeal of English acts in America—the public is always looking for novelty and the *American* public, raised on the stylized accents of the Ronald Colmans and the Vivien Leighs, is always looking for *English* novelty. The show was "Hullabaloo"—and Klein was determined to protect me from being overwhelmed.

In the midst of rehearsals, Klein rushed into my dressing room to inform me that we weren't getting equal time.

"That limey group is getting three songs!" he said in indignation. Everyone was supposed to be limited to two.

"Nah—it can't be. It's in the contract."

"Contract, shmontract. I saw it in the script.

We've got to settle this!" And with that he rushed back to the battlefront.

The war waged on through the day. In the confusion of a television rehearsal, it's often difficult to get to the point. But the word spread as I was waiting for some sort of decision that Vinton was holed up in his room until he got his way. And, meanwhile, Al had complicated the issue by changing the cue cards with a large marking pen he carried around in his hip pocket. It seemed he wasn't satisfied with the billing and had taken things literally into his own hands. When this confusion came to light, the word spread that "Vinton" had tampered with the cue cards. Everything done by anyone associated with me was done by "Vinton." And this was the wrong thing to do with Gary Smith, then and now one of the top TV producers in the world. That first bad impression made it difficult for me to make a mark in TV for years afterward. That's why you didn't see me on too many TV shows in the sixties.

In the middle of everything, my old buddy Speedy Thomas appeared with a tape recorder under his arm. He had always been a great singer, and now that I was back in New York and starring on a hot TV show he guessed it was a great time to make a try at his own career.

"Any other time, Speedy," I apologized; "I'm in the middle of a political situation now and—"

"Just listen to my tapes, Bobby," he insisted.

"Speedy, I love you. We're great buddies. But you just can't walk into a TV studio like this, and right now it's especially bad—"

116

"I get it. I can take a hint," he said before I could explain. And he walked out with a shrug as if to say, Now that you've got it made, you don't have time for your old friends. I haven't heard from Speedy since.

In the depths of my gloom, I asked Al to review everything with me. I couldn't believe something couldn't be worked out. "Give 'em what they want. Apologize. But let's get on with the show. Let 'em sing three songs."

Allen was adamant. "Look at that script—it's in black and white—'Westminster Cathedral,' then 'Segue,' and then 'Georgie Girl.'" That middle word, "Segue," is of course no song at all but a stage direction meaning a transition from one thing to another without interruption.

Al took this little embarrassment in stride and continued to try to shape me into the image of the unapproachable superstar. He edged me onto "The Ed Sullivan Show" by horse trading with its producer Bob Preckt—"I give you this act if you'll take this guy, too." And there it became obvious to me that perhaps I was too young and too naïve to play up to the role Al intended. Frank Sinatra introduced me on that big night, and I was overawed. I didn't feel worthy to be on the same stage, and for that reason I was so tense I gave a strained performance.

I said at the beginning that, for all I know, I might have done as much for Klein as he did for me. It came about because of the peculiarities of the star system in the record business. When the British groups first started to make their invasion of the United States, they came to me, as a proud possessor of

117

several gold records, for advice on what to do with their careers in this country. I advised Mickey Most, the record producer for such acts as Herman's Hermits and the Animals, that they had to have a manager like Allen Klein. When they went back to Britain, they passed on this advice to the Rolling Stones, who told the Beatles. As a result, Al wound up representing some of the hottest new properties ever to be imported to our shores. Before long he had almost an entire floor at the Time-Life Building and he could no longer spend time managing me personally. He had an associate who, he said, would take care of me—and even this decision worked out pleasantly for me. Al must have guessed that I couldn't have been associated with a man more to my liking than Pete Bennett.

Allen Klein and I never had a written contract. We lasted so long, and were so good for each other, probably because we didn't need a contract. Al Klein moved into my life with a handshake and out of it the same way.

THIRTEEN
Forty Guys with Baseball Bats

If we only understood what makes people tick, we wouldn't make half the mistakes we do. We wouldn't yell at our kids because the boss ignored us. We wouldn't be suspicious of our friends when they compliment us. We wouldn't become tigers behind the wheel of a car when the stock market goes down. But for some reason our marvelous educational system teaches us very little about motivation and behavior. And we build invisible screens around ourselves, thinking no one can interpret our intentions and emotions and not attempting to decipher the feelings of others.

Nothing else can explain why some people are habitually late, or why otherwise mild-mannered individuals scowl and curse when a windshield separates them from a pedestrian. One of the blessings of my wide-ranging career—a broad battlefront on which I have some advances and some reverses every day—is that I have been able to experience more ups and downs with *people* than I could have any other way. For my business is 99 percent dependent on the likes and dislikes, the desires and needs of people.

As is usually the case, I have learned more from my mistakes than from my successes. A failure at least shows you what went wrong; a success you're likely to attribute to a hundred good things you'd like to believe about yourself.

For a long time I thought that first film I made, *Surf Party*, wasn't such a bad picture for what it was. When we were living in New York I rented a print of it and would show it off to friends who stopped in. Then I forgot about it and before I knew what had happened I got an enormous bill for overdue charges. I had to give it back fast. But I decided to show it one last time for all the kids in the neighborhood. I threw a party, with popcorn, cake, and ice cream and had a great turnout. Just as I put the first reel on, I got a long-distance phone call. Half an hour later I returned to my basement studio to find the kids drifting out. Soon the place was empty, except for one staunch figure sitting right up in front of the screen. It was my German shepherd. Even more surprising, he watched through to the bitter end. I don't know if the picture was all that bad, but the next day, as I was putting the film back in the cans to ship it off, my dog bit me right in the seat of the pants.

Lesson number one: hope for the best in people but expect the worst.

About this time I was introduced to movie impresario Joe Levine, and I looked for big things to happen. He asked me to sing the "Lonely Girl" theme in his film on Jean Harlow. Later, Dolly and I were Joe's guests on his yacht, and talk turned to movie possibilities. He had a script that was somewhat advanced for its time, a love story involving a young man in an affair with a woman twice his age. I asked Klein what he thought. It's not for you, he said; this kid runs off with a hippie to Berkeley, and your image is just the opposite. He told Joe Levine that I didn't think I was interested in *The Graduate*.

Lesson number two: don't get type-cast.

In a sense I was also type-cast as a promoter, a hustler, who would do anything to make an impression. I was to meet Levine on another occasion in midtown Manhattan; there was still talk of some kind of a movie deal. As I was waiting for his car in front of the Time-Life Building in Rockefeller Center, a crowd of teen-agers from an out-of-town bus gathered around me, asking for autographs and creating quite a stir. When Joe arrived he was impressed by that kind of importance with the general public. But it was also obvious he thought I had set the whole thing up.

Lesson number three: don't push too hard too soon.

Because I had done the theme from *Harlow*, I was offered the chance to sing "Raindrops Keep Falling on My Head," the Burt Bacharach tune in *Butch Cassidy and the Sundance Kid*. Only price separated me from the producer. The figure for "Raindrops" was quite a bit lower than what I had received for *Harlow*.

I held out for my price, thinking of that other rule that the price you put on your work is how others will value you. "Look, you'll find the extra money," I said, but they didn't.

These are some of the errors in judgment and some of the bad luck that dogged me in my attempts to go beyond the record business. Remember, all this time I was blessed with one gold record after another. Pete Bennett was now my advisor and promoter in the Allen Klein organization, and because of his zany attitude and good humor the successes seemed bigger and the mistakes seemed funnier. Pete looked as if he would be at home in the toughest neighborhoods in Brooklyn as well as in the White House. He was an Italian Pierre Salinger in appearance; he always took the direct approach. Our biggest moment together came when politics crossed my path: I was invited to entertain at Richard Nixon's first inauguration and later to give my views on the problems of the youth of the country.

About this time the college riots were in full swing; tear gas and four-letter words were the opposing weapons. Was there anything people in the entertainment business could do—especially people who had a college-age following? Pete suggested the direct approach: "Look, we get forty guys with baseball bats and put 'em in the back of a truck and drive to the nearest campus where there's a protest. The next day every paper in the country will show what we did. And that'll be the end of that."

"Pete," I said, "I know you mean well, but let's forget it."

Along with entertainers like Tony Bennett and Art Linkletter, I sang the inauguration song, entertained at the various inaugural balls, and met President Nixon in the Oval Office. Pete enjoyed the festivities as much as I did, so much so that he was casting about for a way to prolong his stay in the capital. He could justify only so much promotion of Bobby Vinton to his boss. Fortunately, he struck up a friendship with a character like him by the name of Frank Genduso, who was a member of the White House staff. And, he knew that a promoter like Allen Klein is always the easiest type to promote. So he got Frank to write a letter to him on White House stationery, thanking the Klein organization for the great help they had given the White House through Pete Bennett. Klein was so impressed he wanted to frame the letter. He called Bennett. "Pete, take all the time you need in Washington."

Pete had learned this "innocent letter" trick when he was trying to get a raise from his boss. He went down the street to one of the major record companies or management firms and "borrowed" some stationery. Then he addressed himself a job offer, complete with explicit salary. Sure enough, Klein opened the letter "by accident," and was immediately persuaded to give Pete a little extra money.

I needed all the help I could get from inventive types like Genduso and Bennett to carry me over some rough spots on this trip. Once Dolly and I came back to our hotel room to find everything cleaned out. Fortunately, the clothes I was going to wear that night were still hanging in the closet—but that's all I had

123

left. One afternoon I was sitting poolside at the Shoreham Hotel, one of Washington's finest, when Dolly and I decided to splurge and have dinner on the patio. Some members of my group and the show joined us. Everyone assumes that the star of the show is a millionaire and will always pick up the tab. This time, a dozen or more people gathered in my party, and it began to look as if I'd have to buy dinner. They didn't realize that steaks for everyone would just about wipe out what I was making for the show. Genduso came to my rescue. Without hesitation he went to the kitchen, borrowed a waiter's jacket, and returned to take our orders. He barked his commands to the chefs so confidently that no one questioned him. And when we had all had a marvelous dinner there was no waiter and therefore no check.

The high point of my Washington experience came when I had an opportunity to present my ideas for the youth of the country to the President. It was a thrill to meet him, and to be asked if I had something to contribute. I told him I thought it was too late to change the feelings of kids on the campus. Their ways were set. They would ignore the establishment. "However," I said, "we can do something about the next generation." I suggested to President Nixon that we could do more good for the future by trying to learn something about motivation, and instilling it in children. Then students would understand and respect what motivates parents and policemen and businessmen and "people over thirty."

"And teach this in the schools?" he suggested. "These are the things we're supposed to learn from history, and novels. And that's what our sports programs are all about. That's where character-building is supposed to happen."

"Why not teach it like reading and writing?" I said. "I'd call it humantics." And in that brief meeting I proposed a course like mathematics or geometry or geography, to be taught at the earliest opportunity. After all, almost every state in the union has its own required courses—the history of the state as well as the basics of the three R's. Why not teach kids what jealousy and pride are, how they come up in everyday situations, and what to do about them?

My word "humantics" may not be the most precise term for such a study, but it's a start. Just because our motivations are often complex doesn't mean we can't bring them out in the open, and by any name that's what we're going to have to do to avoid the confrontations we've all seen.

President Nixon listened with full respect to my off-the-cuff program. I'm sure an educator or a child psychologist could have poked holes in my argument. I know that most politicians would have patted me on the head and turned away. But Nixon listened sympathetically. He explained how the federal government couldn't become involved in curriculum—so a direct approach wasn't possible. He referred me to several senators who had an interest in this sort of thing. It was much more than I expected. For the first time in my life I had the feeling that I could contribute something important to the welfare of my fellow man. All of a sudden it hit me: What a meaningless thing it is to sell records, even millions of them! In contrast what a powerful thing it is to be a contributor to the progress of mankind. In a small way, I had received an inkling of that feeling just marching in the army. It was the feeling of being a participant instead of a spectator. When I visited some of the ancient monuments in Rome, I had a sense of what great men have done for the generations that follow them. If you've ever been to the White House or the houses of Congress, you can't escape the impact of the contributions of the great men of our history. But what could I do, a Polish kid from Canonsburg, whose only talent was to make records? Inside me, although I wasn't consciously aware of it at the time, there was a burning desire to do something for my people. The Polish prince, as it were, was waiting to be born.

If I had a full-time lobbyist I might have gotten somewhere with my proposal. I still believe there is merit in "humantics." I know that I have to learn—on my own—why people act the way they do and why their anger or envy or distrust is often only a superficial symbol of something much simpler and more innocent. I hope I'm teaching what I know to my children. But I bring it up here more as a way of saying something about Richard Nixon.

Here is a complex man I knew only briefly. (Meeting people like this is one of the side benefits of being an entertainer. I also briefly met the families of Lyndon Johnson and Gerald Ford.) I also saw Nixon through his children, and, believe it or not, his life didn't begin with Watergate. Before that time he was twice chosen by a heavy majority of Americans of all types to be their President. He was Vice President under a great man. He had to struggle all his life to

126

stay in his chosen field, running for re-election every two years as a Congressman, vying for the governor's office in California, trying to keep one step ahead of his detractors. He knew what it meant to lose, and what it took to come back. In that, I can empathize with him.

And he also managed to make his impact on the world at large. No one man is responsible for the course of international events, but in this man's short term at the helm the Vietnam War ended, China opened a bridge to the West, and a pattern of economic and social cooperation was established with the Soviet Union. I'm out of my depth in arguing foreign affairs; yet no one can deny there was a spirit of cooperation and progress during that period that seems to have stagnated since. I believe historians will someday write that Nixon was a great President, who was set up by an elite political group that needed to discredit him because of his growing popularity.

From time to time I mention Richard Nixon's name on the stage. Invariably, the mere mention of that name brings a hostile attitude from friends. At the other extreme, I see in print some of the most pompous statements from political commentators and academicians about how the nation was tottering on the brink of constitutional collapse when Nixon stood on his claim of personal possession of the infamous tapes. In both cases, I feel the reaction of otherwise normal people to Richard Nixon has something to do with "humantics." The emotional bias these people exhibit is deep-rooted and unthinking. I have to think they're acting like forty guys with baseball bats.

FOURTEEN
Write a Scene for Me and the Kid

As the sixties came to a close I began to feel the need for some fresh air. It's true I should have been satisfied with the way things were going. My popularity as a performer was growing, and so was my family: we were now expecting our fourth child. I was having the time of my life with friends like Pete Bennett. One year I had a record called "Please Love Me Forever" in the top five. But nothing added up to the expectations I had for myself, and the hard-sell approach of the Klein organization wasn't working the way I had hoped.

At my agency, William Morris, I kept getting promises that never seemed to materialize. The agent assigned to me for movies, Stan Kamen, would call with high hopes for a big part for me. "It's down to four guys." "It's down to you and this one other guy."

Then finally, "Next time, Bob; they decided the other guy fit the part just a little better." I began floundering.

Then I got the break I had been looking for. I was playing in Las Vegas when I received a call from Irv Schechter, a colleague of Stan Kamen's at the Morris agency, who was also in the movie field. "John Wayne's son, Mike, saw your picture on a record album," he said, "and he thinks you'd be great as Duke's son in a new movie."

"Is it that easy, Irv?"

"Come over for a test in the morning. They really think you look like one of the family." I took a plane to Los Angeles the next morning, but discovered my appointment had been switched to the late afternoon. I had some time to kill. I decided to do some homework to make sure I'd look like John Wayne's son. First, the hairdresser, for a mod haircut that was more western than Madison Avenue. Then the haberdashery, for a rawhide vest and boots. At four o'clock I walked into the studio office and was introduced to the producer, Mike Wayne—a *real* son of the Duke—and the director, George Sherman. Before I could open my mouth they said in unison, "That's it! You're perfect for the part."

The movie was to be filmed in Durango, Mexico, where John Wayne had a large ranch that was his favorite locale for pictures. I mentioned to Pete Bennett where I was heading. "What a coincidence!" he said. "Up here in Yonkers, where I live, John Wayne, Jr., is opening his nightclub act next week." I could see the wheels turning in Pete's head. What a way to

129

solidify my position with Wayne! Pete and his buddies would give his son a big welcome on opening night, and let it be known that they were friends of Bobby Vinton.

Pete went all out. The champagne flowed and there were standing ovations from his party of rough characters for John Wayne, Jr. They sent a note back to the dressing room and were invited in. "We want to help you out in any way we can," Pete said. "Any time you need something done, you know who you can count on." And he came right to the point. "Next time you're talking to your father, tell him Bobby Vinton's buddies are your buddies."

Down in Durango, there wasn't much to do while we were waiting for the filming to begin. It was a new experience for me, passing the time of day with people like Richard Boone and Duke's leading lady, Maureen O'Hara. There were plenty of opportunities for Wayne to mention something about his son, the singer. One day, while we were playing a card game that was a favorite of ours, liar's poker, I couldn't stand it any longer. "Say, Duke, I hear your son is doing very well in his nightclub act in New York. Some of my friends caught him the other day."

"What son?"

"John Wayne, Jr.," I said.

"Oh yeah—I heard about that guy. I'd better have my lawyers do something about him. There's no Jr. in my family."

"I don't think you'll have to do anything after I tell my friend Pete."

I told the story to Pete, and apparently there was

no need to call in the lawyers, because nothing further was heard from John Wayne, Jr.

Duke had a good laugh over my attempt to ingratiate myself with him. He liked the honesty I showed in telling the whole story; in fact, it's difficult to be anything but honest with a man like Wayne. I studied him closely, looking for faults, because I couldn't believe that the character I had seen on the screen could be so much the same in real life. Maybe that's why we all like to read the gossip columns, searching for shortcomings in the stars to make up for our own. I found that the John Wayne on the screen is no bigger than the John Wayne in person.

He was considerate of everyone on the set. In the hot Durango sun he would go out of his way to offer a drink of water to one of the prop boys as if he were offering it to Maureen O'Hara. He could get along with just about anyone because he didn't put on an act himself. That was his greatest lesson for me: to be a star you don't have to be something you *aren't*. From the time of that first meeting with Wayne, I began to change my approach to my business. Before then, I had always tried to act a role I thought the public wanted. Now I began to be myself, and I began to discover that people like me for what I am.

I don't know what it takes to be a great actor in front of the cameras, but in that film it meant for me to *live* the part. I was gunned down by Richard Boone's desperadoes in the first reel, and did a deathbed scene with my screen mother, Miss O'Hara. Luckily, I had a toothache coming on. I decided to make something of it. Just before I was to arrange myself in a dying pose

131

on the set, I went to the men's room and put cold water right on the aching tooth. I was wincing with pain even before the cameras rolled, and as I turned to my mother to utter my last words a stab of lightning went from my jaw down my neck. That evening, Miss O'Hara called me to say it was one of the most convincing performances she had seen.

Not too long ago I saw the film again as a "movie of the week" on TV. As soon as the scene in Durango unfolded, the feeling came over me that this was really part of my life. I had lived on that ranch! I had known those people! Fortunately, they cut my deathbed scene—perhaps because it was the family hour—which was one part of the film I didn't want to believe was real. The film, by the way, was *Big Jake*.

Wayne mentioned casually that he'd like to have me with him in his next picture. It was the type of polite gesture you expect in the movie business. So I was truly shocked when he called not too long afterward to offer me a part, however small, in his film *The Train Robbers*. He knew it would be a professional sacrifice for me. I would have to go on location for three months, canceling all my performances for that period. I couldn't afford it, but I couldn't resist it, either. If I was ever going to learn the movie business, I had to pay my dues.

You've got to have everybody pulling for you to do your best, and I sensed that the director wanted to bring his own friends into the picture for some of the minor roles. The vibrations weren't right. It's the same thing that gives the home team an advantage over the visiting team in a football or basketball game.

As the filming went into the second month I began to feel that I was being shut out of the picture completely. Wayne picked up on this himself, and went to the director. "Didn't I ask you to write a scene for me and the kid? I'm not going to say it again."

Finally I was handed a script one morning and told the scene would be shot with Wayne and me in the afternoon. "Couldn't you have given it to me last night?" I asked. This was the director's final gesture about how he felt toward me. Rod Taylor, one of the film's leading men, saw what was happening and volunteered his help. Over the lunch hour he coached me in the direction of the story and the reading of my lines. It's the same thing in learning a song—two people can work twice as effectively as one. And when we were on camera, Wayne took his time, making sure we got a perfect take. He told me that if I was seriously interested in pursuing a movie career, this scene with him would help a lot. When the scene was completed, I took him aside. "Duke, you didn't have any more time than I did with the script, and you didn't have any help. You ran through it as if you'd been doing it all your life."

"Well," he drawled, "for forty years."

But my favorite scene from that film never was caught by the cameras. Wayne wasn't feeling all that well; his old friend Bruce Cabot had just passed away. But he agreed to go through with a big outdoor scene even though his heart was heavy. Everything seemed to go well until the director pointed out a truck that had driven into the background in plain view and spoiled the scene. Wayne turned in the direction of

133

the hapless driver, raised his fist high in the air, and was about to cuss him out, when he saw a crowd of sightseers nearby. His mouth formed around his most ferocious invective: "You, you son— you bas— you, you . . ." Finally he bit his lip and yelled, as he felt the sweet, little-old-lady fans watching him, "You stinker!"

As much as I enjoyed these brief episodes in the movies, I realized that, like every other art form, movie-making is not something you dabble in. You've got to put in your apprenticeship. I knew I could walk on a stage and follow the biggest act in the business, but I couldn't walk before a camera and follow the biggest actor. And my agents weren't giving me any encouragement. They were looking, but they weren't sticking their necks out. And the reason for that went back to an early episode I had over a TV role.

Stan Kamen had confidence in me as an actor before I had done anything except the old *Surf Party* film. He put his reputation on the line by recommending me for a part in an Alfred Hitchcock drama; well-respected agents like Stan are trusted in the business for their judgment. The director routinely asked me what was the last movie or TV part I had done. Naïvely, I said this was my first. "What makes you think you can do it? Do you think it's fair to the rest of us?" he asked. I told him I was confident, after appearing publicly almost all my life, that I could handle the role. But then I learned that this was a big test for him, too, as a director. His career depended on coming through with flying colors in this assignment.

134

Reluctantly, he ran through a rehearsal. I was to put on a happy-go-lucky manner, he said, even though I had just received some bad news. "All right," he announced, "we'll run through it for the cameras in an hour." After the break, I noticed several people standing around with the director who hadn't been there before. As I began to run through my part, I heard the director whispering in the background. "Why's he doing that? He's acting happy-go-lucky in a painful situation." Suddenly the director asked everybody to take a break. Kamen called with disturbing news.

"They're replacing you with Jack Cassidy, Bob."

"Hey, I just saw him on the set. How'd he get here so fast?"

"They want an experienced actor. Sorry."

My head was spinning for weeks. I couldn't believe what had happened. It was a long time before it occurred to me that I *had* followed the director's instructions and hadn't misplayed the part. I had been ambushed. And the net result was that Kamen had stuck his neck out for me once and wouldn't do it again. He couldn't afford to in this business.

Occasionally he would call with the same old story. "It's down to you and this one other guy." Then, "They just felt he fit the part a little better. Sorry." Finally, one day Stan exalted: "I've got something for you—entertaining the troops in Vietnam."

"What does it mean now?" I asked. "The war is about over."

"Are you interested? There are still some boys

135

over there whom we seem to have forgotten about."

"Okay, Stan. I'll do anything you say." At last, I thought, he had something for me.

But then he said, "Bob, it's down to you and this one other guy. . . ." Sure enough, two days later, they picked the other guy—for Vietnam. I was beginning to learn how bad things were for me. They didn't even want me in Vietnam.

During this period I kept searching for the right direction in my professional life, knowing in my heart that there was something calling me, something larger than a career even in the movies or than another gold record. John Wayne and Maureen O'Hara convinced me a good manager could help. I was recommended to one of the biggest—Dick Linke, who was handling people like Jim Nabors and Andy Griffith. And I decided that the fresh air I sought was in Southern California. We went house-hunting in Los Angeles.

Dolly and I were met by a real estate agent, Thelma Orloff, who quickly punctured some of our balloons. When I mentioned how much we were willing to spend, a six-figure amount that I thought would buy a castle in 1970, she didn't even look up from her desk. She took us for a drive out to San Fernando Valley, but this wasn't my idea of California. "I want water, mountains, air!" I said. "Let's see Beverly Hills." So we looked at one movie star's mansion after another. Dolly got lost in Paul Newman's closet. Still we didn't see what I wanted. We went back to New York.

The next time I had to come to Los Angeles, I looked out the airplane window as we circled in over

L.A. International and saw an exciting ridge with a few scattered houses on it. I asked Thelma again to take us house-hunting.

"There's nothing up there," she said.

"Turn here," I answered. "That's where I was looking from the plane."

We pursued a conventional suburban street for a mile or so and finally came to a brick wall overgrown with shrubbery. "Here," I said. It turned out to be the former estate of Cary Grant, and before him Douglas Fairbanks, Jr. I immediately took a liking to it, with its sprawling Spanish architecture and country-like atmosphere. Below us lay Santa Monica bay. Against Thelma's advice, I peeked in the living room window, and that's all I needed. It was priced well beyond our means, but I knew it was the kind of place the person I wanted to be would live. To me it was a castle. We scraped together all the money we had, and borrowed the rest. Our friends thought we had gone crazy. All the ties we had made in New York were broken, our future was mortgaged. I discovered that Dick Linke couldn't devote his personal time to my career, and had to turn me over, once again, to an assistant, Dick Lane.

The pressure began to mount. Our fourth child was born; Dolly had to undergo several serious operations. I felt I was losing touch with the business, and decided to be my own manager for a change. We weren't able to sell our house in New York. I remembered how, at another crisis in my life, when I was just starting out as a teen-age bandleader, I broke out in hives. Once, at the end of a dance we had given, I

137

remember the organizer of the affair saying to Joe Dybell, "My, what a strange-looking bandleader you have." I was learning, all over again, that no matter what the strain, it's a great feeling to have to depend on yourself. We had three things: a new baby, a new home, and a new life. Something was going to happen.

It was just like the movies.

FIFTEEN
The Fan Club

I was on "The Tonight Show" with Sammy Davis, Jr., a long while back, when I still lived in New York, and was casually talking with him backstage when a page announced, "Your fan club members are here." Sammy turned and started walking over to a handsome black couple approaching us. But they walked right past him and shook hands with me, to Sammy's consternation.

They were Julia and Tony Walker, who had organized a fan club for me when I thought that fan clubs were only a collection of teen-age girls who wanted autographed pictures. I first met them when I went with my father to give a show at the old Freedomland, in the Bronx. I noticed a group of people near the stage who seemed to be having a great time at this open-air show, with the whole family gathered around

139

picnic baskets clapping to the music. Afterward, they asked me if I wanted some chicken. They were warm, outgoing, hardworking New Yorkers, several families of various races and nationalities. I called them the Freedomlanders.

I would be hard put to explain exactly what the magnetism is between us. We both like the same kind of music; we like to spend our leisure time the same ways. Our relationship is symbiotic: they need me as a link to the whole backstage world of show business.

Fan club members go to record stores to make sure they're stocking my latest hits. They send out newsletters informing each other where I'll be appearing. They spend their vacations following me around the country to attend my performances. Whether I have a good night or a bad one, they're out there cheering me on, or consoling me with home-cooked food afterward. The Guinness Book of Records should include the fact that a Mrs. Weekly in Florida has seen more than two hundred of my shows. It's not unusual to receive a hundred gifts backstage on my birthday.

In return, I sometimes introduce them in the audience, send them notes when I'm in their area, and welcome them whenever I can after a show. And whenever I sing something with real meaning and have to focus on someone to tell my story to, I think of all of them.

I suppose every performer has a fan club something like the "Freedomlanders." What I think is special about mine is that they had more faith in me than I did when things weren't looking so bright. Now, I said at the very beginning that I've never had a come-back if you consider my professional life as a whole. I've grown a little each year. But I've had great emotional ups and downs, setbacks in one area or another, and losses in popularity in one medium or another. And when I wasn't making gold records anymore, I told Julia one day, "Let's drop the fan club. Let's face it—I'm not a hit."

"Are you kiddin'?" she answered. "You're just startin' to roll!" They stuck with me because they believed there was something more to me than "Roses Are Red." Their favorite line was, "One day you'll do something."

Julia is president of what we now call the "international" club. In Chicago there's the "booster" club. And in Los Angeles the "correspondence" club. There are so many names worthy of mention that I hesitate to start for fear of leaving someone out.

One of the important functions of a fan club is to give objective feedback on performances and record albums. After a show they're likely to tell me that my female vocalist Carol Jolin couldn't be heard, or that the revolving ball that throws lights all over the room should be used in the big-band numbers rather than during a reprise of my hit songs. They take pictures and advise me on what pictures and titles I should use in new albums. As Mrs. Weekly says, and she should know, every performance is different, every audience is different. Or, as I put it, performing is like making love—to a different person each night.

For a show that runs for a week, which is common, I usually do two performances an evening—at

141

eight and midnight. In some communities, I make those times much earlier so the family can come. There aren't many performers who appeal to both families and "swingers." Each show is carefully planned to fit the mood of the audience. And I also try to take advantage of the special talents of the musicians; I bring only my vocalists, my drummer and sometime leader, Lloyd Morales, and Vinnie Carbone, who makes all the necessary arrangements. If the trumpet section is particularly strong, I select music to feature them. But I don't need more than a few loyal people to travel with me on the road. All my life a few good friends have been more support than an army of onlookers.

Whether I'm appearing at Las Vegas or the Mill Run in Chicago, I go in a day ahead, if I can, and check the previous entertainer, if possible, to see what's working for him. The morning of the first day, I set up the whole stage, moving things around myself if necessary. I pay special attention to the sound; I'm not content to be as good as the last guy. For long hours we rehearse in the afternoon. By six o'clock I'm exhausted, and the first show is at eight. So on the first night I may look preoccupied with a dozen different things: the third trumpet hit a C instead of a B flat, there's feedback in the mike, that speaker's breaking. . . . I'm an integral part of everything on the stage, and everything must be right.

Sometimes a fan will say afterward, "You didn't sing 'He' tonight. It would have worked." Onstage I'm constantly weighing decisions like that: is the crowd too high for a religious number, or will it only confuse

142

them? Or a fan will say, "You weren't in the audience very long tonight." TV producer Pierre Cassette once told me he came to one of my shows and looked for me on the tops of booths and in the aisles. "I could hear you, Bobby, but I couldn't see you. Then I looked on the stage—and you were there for a change."

A fan club as intimate as this is one of the reasons why I've been able to go to some of the smallest communities in the "old country" part of the United States and always have a nucleus of supporters on hand. And on more than one occasion the "Walker Connection" has saved me from perilous situations. The case of the "Tree Lady" immediately comes to mind.

At one of my shows in New York, several years after I had met the Walkers, a group of lively people near the stage requested "Tie a Yellow Ribbon on the Old Oak Tree." As we will see, that song has bittersweet memories for me—but if there is one thing I will always do, it's comply with any reasonable request. I soon discovered the reason for the request: a vivacious woman leaped up on the stage and began to join in the act. Her body was encased in a brown burlap tube, yellow ribbons encircled her waist, and leafy branches sprouted from her arms and head. She *was* the song. I went along with the gag and hammed it up with her.

The same thing happened the following night, and then a third time. On each occasion the woman became more uninhibited; I checked the group she was with to make sure an irate husband wasn't looking on with disapproval. I saw him—but he was clapping with enthusiasm. So as not to let the situation get out of hand, I invited the couple backstage and explained my attitude toward this form of audience participation.

"You're wonderful to go to all this trouble," I said.

She and her husband told me they were great admirers of me, and they'd do anything to help me. Then he opened his coat to reveal a shoulder holster with the biggest revolver I have ever seen. "Look," he said in a confidential tone, "I'm sort of a private eye, and guns are something of a hobby with me. If you ever have any trouble with anyone, call on me."

"Sure," I said, taking his card timidly. "But I've never had any problem—"

"You never know, right?"

Two weeks later, I was preparing to go downstairs at the Palmer House, in Chicago, for the second show of the evening, when I received a breathless call from Julia Walker. "It's the tree lady, Bobby—she's coming to Chicago tonight and she wants to travel with you as your "Tree Lady."

"Nah, don't worry. I talked to her and her husband and they're okay."

"Really, this is serious!" she insisted. "The Tree lady is coming to Chicago. She wants to travel with you as your tree."

I called the show room at once to try to head off my pursuer. "There's a 'tree' that might come to the show tonight," I explained with growing panic, "a tree lady."

"What's that!"

144

"A woman dressed like a tree. Don't let her in—no matter what!"

"Mr. Vinton, can you describe her a little better?" There was a decidedly skeptical tone in his voice.

"A Tree lady—you know, green arms, brown body, leaves around her head—"

"I see. Well, we'll certainly keep on the lookout, Mr. Vinton."

I surveyed the room carefully before I stepped out onstage. The tree lady wasn't in evidence. During the show a few people entered at the back of the room, and I almost missed my cues, but there was nothing leafy in the audience. The show went on and the security guards told me that there was nothing to be concerned about. After the show, I insisted on using the back elevator. But when the back door opened on the sixteenth floor, there she was. I knew that if anyone wants to get you there's no place to hide.

I asked, "Where's your husband?" picturing in graphic detail the huge revolver in his shoulder holster.

"He's at home."

"That's where *you* belong. Now, go back to your husband. I don't need a tree lady. Now, let's remain friends, and keep our daydreams for the stage." So we talked it out, and as far as I know the tree lady and the private eye lived happily ever after.

I hope.

Sixteen
The Storm
Before the Calm

One of the good things that happens to you when you're not "knockin' 'em dead" is that you listen more carefully to your critics, and you discover who really believes in you. The fan clubs seemed to get stronger as the times became stormier. They weren't fair-weather friends. And even when the crowds weren't there, the newspaper people were talking about how I would do something, someday, bigger than drawing crowds.

On one occasion in those early seventies I remember a particularly good opening night at the Palmer House in Chicago. Critics Aaron Gold and Irv Kupcinet wrote about a talent they saw in me to go on to something better. A few nights later, I came down to an audience of twelve people. I volunteered to buy them all a steak dinner, but one of them explained she

146

had come a long distance. I couldn't desert one of my fan club members; I put on a full show, and enjoyed it!

Almost every entertainer has nights like that. It hurts only when it gets in the papers. About that same time I opened to an enthusiastic crowd at the Waldorf Astoria in New York. That was the night my daughter Kristin stole the show singing "Daddy's Little Girl." Later in the week, critic Jack O'Brien stopped by to see the show and discovered only twenty people there; when he duly reported it, my chances of a big revival in the Big Apple seemed to be gone forever. Little did I know that my next appearance there would be to a sold-out house at—Carnegie Hall.

In this turbulent period I kept looking for an opening in the clouds. Like everybody else, I wanted some sort of security, not exactly in money, but in recognition. Even though I had two hits about this time—"Every Day of My Life" and "Sealed with a Kiss"—I never knew what to expect on the road. Once I took my mother with me for a show in Sharon, Pennsylvania—my kind of country. Backstage, she chided me for pouring a glass of Dubonnet. "You shouldn't drink so much wine," she said. "It isn't good for you." I told her I occasionally had a glass before a show that wasn't well attended, because it made the house look full. She peeked out through the curtains and saw, as I expected, only a few hundred people in the large auditorium. "How're we doing tonight, Mom?" I asked.

"Here," she said immediately, pouring me a full glass, "you're going to need this tonight!"

Not long after, I was driving to a nightclub for a

performance that had all the earmarks of another disaster. The promoters had told me that they had sold only a hundred tickets. But as I approached the unfamiliar location I could see, from the highway, a full parking lot right next to the club. Things are picking up, I thought; the worst is over. I said to the promoter, "Looks like the crowd's going to be good tonight."

"Don't get all excited," he replied. "We're located next to a junkyard."

When everything seemed to be going wrong, a sort of brash confidence remained with me. I always felt I would have my own TV show some day. I knew that there were a lot of people on my side. Like the time I almost lost my prize clarinet, the one my father first taught me on (and the one *he* learned on). I was doing a show at a Miami Beach hotel when someone made off with my old clarinet. Something had to be done fast: I was afraid that by the time I reported it to the police it would be out of the country. So I went to the "little guys," the waiters and busboys. It's a keepsake, I told them. It's not worth fifty dollars to any fence, but it's worth a million dollars to me. Two hours later, a waiter brought it to my room, no questions asked.

Lloyd Morales, my current drummer, joined me during my stormy days. Lou Carto had been with me for eight years but felt it was time to leave. Things were indeed stormy. Lloyd and I shared many funny experiences waiting for the calm to come. At our first meeting, in fact, we were so engrossed in conversation, waiting to board our plane, that we didn't notice we were in a crowd of people seeing their friends off.

We were impressed with each other—he had played with Lee Brown and other performers, and I had several gold records under my belt. Each of us was looking to follow the other one's lead. Suddenly I got the sensation that the airport was moving. But it was the plane, taking off with our orchestra. And it took a while for Lloyd to realize that the Bobby Vinton fans were real, and not just the invention of a public relations man. On his first show in Augusta, Georgia, I gave him instructions about security along with all the other details of lighting and sound, but he must have thought I was joking. After the show, we were relaxing in the dressing room when there came a pounding at the door. He had heard all the stories about women rushing up the aisles with albums to autograph, but he thought I was exaggerating. He opened the door and he was overrun by overly enthusiastic fans. Lloyd actually had to call the police to restore order. That was something he wasn't used to in the entertainment business.

By the way, if I had to do it all over again, I would take a leaf out of the book of my young contemporaries. I would invest more time and money in preparations. Then, I had a one-man organization. As good as Lloyd was, he couldn't handle everything by himself.

Recently, I've added a righthand man to my organization—Vinnie Carbone—who played sax with the Glenn Miller band at the age of seventeen. His experience has been of invaluable help to me, especially after my father, my unofficial manager and confidant, passed away.

When things aren't going well for entertainers in this country, it's customary for them to seek their fortune abroad. Many a singer has ridden on his popularity in Europe for years after his decline in the U.S.A. It was tempting, therefore, for me to accept a series of performances in Caracas, Venezuela, especially since my records had already sold well here for years.

Dolly was now pregnant with our fifth child, so we decided to make a little vacation out of the trip for both of us. We were met at the airport by a very hospitable press. It's customary, of course, for a singer to maintain the appearance of being single and available, even though his fans know he's married. But at this press conference, there was no hiding the fact that Dolly was expecting. We discussed our family, and the photographers had a field day taking our pictures together. The press asked me if by showing my wife I felt I would lose popularity. I said, "No, it didn't hurt Presley or Tom Jones." That evening I had dinner with the president of my record company in Venezuela. "Please Love Me Forever" was the biggest record in the country at the time. "Do you realize," he said, "you're the number one male singer down here?"

"Bigger than Tom Jones or Elvis Presley?" I asked in amazement.

"Oh yeah," he answered knowingly. "Those guys are all married!"

"Wait'll you see the papers in the morning!" I laughed.

I could do no wrong, however, in South America. I had been warned that my patented act—going out into the crowd and playing up to the women—would go against the grain of the *macho* Latins. I ventured into the audience gingerly, but quickly discovered, once again, that people are people the world over. People like to be serenaded, and men take it as a compliment when their women are treated with friendly affection. Perhaps they want to identify with me. In any case, one small lesson was beginning to sink in: I could appeal to a wide variety of ethnic and cultural backgrounds. I had yet to realize the simple fact staring me in the face: I had entertained in about every major language but my native Polish!

I didn't know what I was looking for. Whatever I promoted most seemed to fall the flattest. When I was doing opening acts for Don Rickles in Las Vegas, I spent most of my fee trying to upgrade my band and impress the people who mattered. Once I had a whole string section added to my aggregation, at the cost of my salary, because I knew Frank Sinatra was a friend of Rickles' and would stop in to see him open. The more violins you have the more important you look as a singer. That particular night, however, Frank got lucky at the tables and was delayed getting to our show. Just as I finished my act, in he came. He looked up at the array of violins and said, "Wow! Rickles must be doing pretty good for himself with a band like that!"

After paying for the strings and doing some gambling, after five weeks in Las Vegas doing seventy straight shows, I went home broke.

SEVENTEEN
Moja Droga,
Ja Cie Kocham

When I first played a tape of "My Melody of Love" in my studio at home, I looked up at the ceiling and said, "Joe, knock with your crutch if you think it's a hit." And I think I could picture a tear forming on Joe Gorlack's cheek. At least I wanted to believe that my one-legged miner from Canonsburg was still with me in spirit.

I had made my way to the top in Las Vegas. And now I had invested everything I had in my quest for another big record. I didn't know yet that I was in search of something bigger than a record.

So far, only Al Gallico had told me he saw something in my Polish song. To seven major record companies it was the biggest Polish joke of all. But Al has been listening to songs all his life—with a special ear. He has an instinct for knowing what songs work with what singers. He goes back as far as the "Papa Loves Mambo" he found for Perry Como. So when he said he was going to see Jay Lasker at ABC Records first thing in the morning, I thought, "Bob Morgan and Bobby Vinton and Joe Gorlack, there's still hope!"

Al is the type of guy who tells people what to do once he's made up his mind. He told Lasker he was going to play a record for him that the seven other major companies had ignored. When it was over, Lasker called me. "We'll sell two million of this."

"Two million! I'll take a million," I gasped. "I'll take ninetieth on the charts—I'll take anything."

"No, we're going to sell two million." The record went into production in August of that year. Lasker opened his annual sales convention that summer by telling his salesmen they were going to sell two million copies of the "Melody of Love" single. The salesmen looked at each other as if to say, "If the boss says we're going to sell two million, it must be good. We're going to sell two million." This is the most basic truth of salesmanship—believing in what you are going to do as if you can see the future in a crystal ball. You don't hope you can do something—you *know* you can.

But when you're dealing with the greatest unknown quantity in the world—the public taste— you've got to have more than salesmanship. No manufacturer can force a product down the throats of Americans. Sam Goldwyn was right: when you know what the public wants, it's already too late. The public tells you what it wants by its own secret ballot, the cash register. So even though Al Gallico and Jay Lasker thought "My Melody of Love" was a winner,

153

we now put our heads to the task of bringing it to the attention of the public.

Jay Lasker and I were in agreement that the record had its primary appeal to Polish people. I hadn't written it with anything more complicated in mind. Its refrain was *"Moja droga, ja cie kocham"*—"My dearest, I love you." Almost every other nationality was represented by a song in the English language with a few words in the native tongue: "C'est Si Bon," "Auf Wiedersehn," "Besame Mucho," "Volare," to name a few. This was the first attempt at a popular song with a few Polish words. I hoped it would come up to the expectations of my mother when she said, "Write a song for the Polish people and they'll love you forever."

We concentrated on distributing and promoting the record in the big metropolitan centers of the Midwest and North where there were large Polish populations. I went to CKLW in Detroit and played disc jockey for a morning. I proclaimed it "Polish Day," and talked in the Polish language between spinning records. The station thought it was an interesting novelty and agreed to continue playing "My Melody of Love." I went next to Cleveland and WIXY, where the same routine went over well. Everyone seemed to think it was more than a gimmick; the song had a strong melody, and the words had what Joe Gorlack had called the human touch.

The following week my record company reported that nothing was happening with the record in either city. It was in the stores, but there was no reaction from buyers. I called a good Polish friend at WIXY,

154

Marge Bush, to make sure the station was still playing the record. She assured me they were. When two weeks went by with no sales, I said to Marge, "I can't believe it! I would have bet my life that record would appeal to people. If I can't make it in Detroit and Cleveland, I'm not going to make it." Then I asked her *when* they were playing the record.

"Oh, at five in the morning and ten at night," she answered. All of a sudden I got a wave of hope. I knew I had a chance, because those hours were good for a lot of records, but not for something my people listened to. Those weren't working men's hours. I checked Buffalo, another center of Polish people. Station WGR had started playing it there and the stores were reporting some action. WKBW, a rocker in contact with other similar stations around the country, started getting reports from local stores. "Melody" was outselling other records three to one, but the station considered it a fluke and didn't report it on their charts. Then it jumped to six to one, then ten to one. Since they hadn't reported it at all, they couldn't list it as number one on the charts, so they ranked it twenty-two one week and then gave it number one the following week. I had broken through the first barrier.

It's easy to criticize a system in which no one plays anything but the top 20 or 30 records and when it keeps your records off the air—that's what has happened to a lot of good young talent since the spectre of payola inhibited the record stations. All the pop music stations and rockers are in touch with one another, and when something new happens in one location all the rest sit up and take notice. So now the system was on my side. Everybody was talking about what was happening in Buffalo. Detroit and Cleveland immediately begin spinning "Melody" more often. Still, no one wants to look foolish in this business, and the Polish lyrics still puzzled the disc jockeys. Some stations told me they'd never play it—it was just a Polish fluke! I went to Chicago, where there are some three million Polish people, and couldn't believe that the stations still didn't want to stick their necks out. Only Ed Schwartz at WIND had the courage to put it on. Because he was the first, I promised him I'd give him a gold record if it sold a million copies.

Gradually, "My Melody of Love" crept into first place on the charts from coast to coast. The holdouts who had sworn they wouldn't play the "gimmick" now were forced by the pressure of the charts to start giving it a spin. In two months, Jay Lasker's prediction was coming true. I was beginning to enjoy the benefits of the top-twenty syndrome. And there on the walls of station WIND, in Ed Schwartz's office, I hung a gold record.

The Polish people had given me that first response that's so necessary to bring a record to the attention of a station. They had gone to the stores to buy it and had called the stations to play it. With that base, "Melody" was then able to come into its own as a song pure and simple. It was music that people of all nationalities wanted to hear.

The unlikely success story of "Melody of Love" would be nothing but the story of another record that happened to catch the public's fancy—except for two

156

things. First, it was a new concept in popular music: it had an unspoken message of social importance, which I'll come to in a minute. And second, it was so interwoven with everything else I was doing that it moved my life forward all along the front—like the ocean suddenly lifting a row of surfers onto their boards.

This last point is perhaps the real moral of my second chance. I believed so much that I was going to make a breakthrough *somewhere* that I had set all the other wheels in motion. I had taken some long-shot bets on myself. Before "My Melody of Love" became a hit, I had been struggling to maintain a good lineup of shows around the country. I had lost some of my attraction with promoters as a result of not having a record on the top twenty. Even in my home country, Pittsburgh, with friends in the press like George Anderson, I couldn't find a promoter who would back my show. Lenny Litman, a big promoter, said he was afraid to take a chance with me in concert because I had played the club circuit all these years and that's how people would view me. So I committed myself a year in advance by putting a deposit on Heinz Hall there, knowing I would have to run my own ads and handle my own ticket-sale promotion. I believed that when the time came around I would be back in the public's fancy, one way or another. My Polish song went to number one just before my appearance in Pittsburgh, and I sold out Heinz Hall for nine straight shows. And I have now appeared for fifteen straight years as a major attraction in that city so close to my heart.

When I came back for a second year of my contract at the Flamingo in Las Vegas, "My Melody of Love" was reaching its peak. My one-time manager Dick Lane was now the talent buyer at the hotel. We joked about how he once couldn't give me away on the Strip, and now I was a headliner with a pay scale to match. Largely because of the hit record, I found my shows had been sold out four weeks in advance. When I told my agent Lee Salomon about this, he was taken aback. "How can that be?" he asked. "People aren't even in town yet and they've bought out your show?" I could hardly believe it myself, but that was the magic of a Polish song.

Ironically, at the conclusion of this very successful run, Dick Lane informed me my option for the following year wouldn't be picked up by the Flamingo. For a few days I was in shock. Dick explained that the reasons would all come out in the wash someday. I knew the Flamingo was going to close, and perhaps they thought I wasn't strong enough yet to be a headliner at the Hilton, the larger hotel under the same ownership. That meant they would have no place to put me. But even this apparent setback turned out to be a blessing in disguise.

There was a PR man at the Riviera, Tony Zoppi, who was something of a scout for their talent buyer, Eddie Torres. Tony was a good friend and had been trying to work something out for years to get me booked at his place. I was just recovering from the shock of my cancellation at the Flamingo when Tony asked me to have lunch with him. "When're you going to work for us?" he asked, as he had done many times before.

"You won't believe this," I replied, "but I've just been turned loose by the Flamingo." It's customary for a headliner to maintain an allegiance to a single Las Vegas club in any one year. This gave the Riviera and Eddie Torres the opening they were looking for. I signed with them for more money than I had ever hoped for. All of a sudden, everybody wanted me. The Hughes organization called. Baron Hilton couldn't believe I had left the Flamingo until I told him they had left me, not the other way around. When Eddie Torres and the Riviera made a move, everybody took notice, because they had the reputation for spotting the coming trends and picking up hot new talent.

And the frosting on the cake came in an offer from the showroom at the MGM Grand. On short notice they had an opening for two weeks. Torres could have held me to my contract and prevented me from taking this plum, but he is as considerate as he is shrewd. He told me I couldn't pass up a chance like that. So I worked the MGM Grand for two big weeks, and the Riviera before and after. In the space of a single season, I had done what few, if any, performers have: headlined in three major Las Vegas hotels.

All this time, "Melody" was spinning on the turntables of America and the Polish words were saying something different from just another lament of a lost love. Those five words were speaking out for ethnic groups of all kinds. The Irish, the Italians, the Latin Americans saw a declaration of pride in "My Melody of Love" that had nothing to do with the words. It had to do with the courage to stand up to

159

popular ridicule. And this is why I know that some critics of the song are way off base. Some said I used the Polish words as a *wedge* to open a new market for a record. Some wedge! In fact, the Polish words were a handicap freely undertaken; and that's why ethnic groups of all kinds found courage in them. Others claimed it was just a catchy tune. My first manager, Allen Klein, in all seriousness told me I should have recorded the lyrics in French, because it was a more romantic language! It would have given me a sexier image, he said, and would have made my career more lasting.

But I was only beginning to discover that there was a power in such a simple concept that would change my whole idea of entertainment.

EIGHTEEN
Mothers, Apple Pie, and Bobby Vinton

Reporters and critics are naturally skeptical about anything that the public likes. But they *can* be won over. When something becomes popular, they start poking around to find out what need it fulfilled, what weakness, perhaps, it catered to. So they approached "Melody" with the idea that it was some pleasant accident, on the one hand, or some devious trick, on the other. When they heard it sung, however, and saw how people responded to it in person, they warmed to my evaluation: it's a song that *means* something to people.

One musicologist told me, "It's so simple and natural it must have been written off the cuff."

I thought about that for a minute. "Let's see, it came from my heart, and I wear my heart on my sleeve, so you're right—it was off the cuff." And it did

161

come from many places inside me, it expressed things I had to talk to someone about. But surely no one knows all his motivations and the sequence of all his feelings. When I talk with my audience, people want to know who the person is that inspired this outpouring. Was it my wife, an old flame, a childhood sweetheart? I try to tell the story at the end of the show. My love, so wrapped up in that melody that it bursts out in the language of my childhood, Polish, is a symbol of many loves. Here is what it has become as I tell it on stage:

I'm looking for a place to go
So I can be all alone
From thoughts and memories . . .
So that when the music plays
I don't go back to the days
When love was you and me.

That's a feeling we all have—the heartache of a love from the past that keeps coming back, when a song stirs a memory. The lyrics continue simply to underline the feeling of loss:

I wish I had a place to hide
All my sorrow, all my pride—
I just can't get along . . .
'Cause the love once so fine

Keeps hurtin' all the time—
Where did I go wrong?

As in any popular song, there's a compromise
here between easy-to-understand words and
thoughts, and anything novel or rich in expression.
The lyrics of even the best songs can go only so far into
real poetry. But there's no missing the point of this
verse. At the lowest ebb of his regrets he sings *"Moja
droga, ja cie kocham."* The Polish words are a cry
from his past—the expression is so basic it can come
out only in the language of his father and his father's
father. So I explain that this love lament can mean just
about anything to you, but to me it has become the
story of my loss of my audience. I don't mind telling
everyone that I had been slipping into obscurity, as
my fans had grown up and gone to other things. And I
did want to go away and hide, so as not to see and hear
the things that reminded me of the days when I was
loved by an audience. My *"moja droga"* was a call
back to them. So you see, I tell the audience, if you
really want to know who my melody of love is—it's
you.

I tell this story with good-natured jokes at my
own expense—"I was so unknown that even American
Express wouldn't consider me for their ad campaign of
ordinary unknowns." And I did miss my audience—
that sentiment was subconsciously true when I wrote
it. The audience responds with a warmth of feeling
I've never had for any other song or story.

163

The mere fact that I had the audacity to make a Polish line the theme of a popular song—when Polish jokes were becoming embarrassingly like slurs—is what rallied ethnic groups of all kinds behind me. Remember, I didn't spout something like "We have a lot to be proud of—let's hear it for our heroes." I did what heroes are supposed to *do*. I stood against the popular tide. I stood up and said, "Count me!" Now, if I had sung something in French or Italian or even Gaelic, it would have been just another lyric trick— something for the sake of variety. As Klein says to this day, maybe in French it would have been a nice romantic song. But that isn't what I wanted to do. I wanted to *say* something.

So I'm not ashamed to accept the accolades that have fallen on me from serious people. I ran out of wall space in my office for all the plaques and citations, all the keys to the city, all the statues and paintings that have come from admirers of "My Melody of Love." What they most admire, I think, is that this expression of ethnic pride didn't come from a poet or historian or organization set up to promote something, but from a kid from Smith Street in Canonsburg. I never knew there were so many Polish organizations until they came out to greet me. I never knew there were some sixty million Americans who can trace some Polish heritage in their backgrounds, until the U.S. Census Bureau told me.

The small point I was able to make is that to be an American means, among other things, to be different and to be proud you're different. In the past, we've often been asked not to be different, to submerge our cultural backgrounds. After the song became a popular success, disc jockeys would come up to me and "confess," as they put it, that they were Polish. They had changed their names. It's more difficult to change your age or to change the color of your skin.

In America, for some reason, we have created a market for products to make us look younger, whiter, straighter. But more and more people in this country are taking pride in being unconventional, in being old, in being nonwhite. Ronald Reagan tells people who ask him if he's too old to be President that in China they think he's too young. If my Polish song contributed anything to this trend, it showed people that they can take pride in their ethnic background as well as in their age, race, color, religion, or economic condition.

I want my children to grow up looking forward to being adults, to being "over thirty," to moving into positions of respect as elders. When someone reaches his fiftieth birthday, we should be able to congratulate him, and come right out and say, "You're a hero! You made it!" Because I've been popular with the public over a long period of time, I've run up against the consciousness of age quite often. After the success of "Melody," I began to fill the bigger auditoriums again. One bleak winter day I was coming into Providence on a half-empty jet when a balding businessman across the aisle introduced himself gingerly. "Pardon me, but aren't you Bobby Vinton?"

"That's right," I said, and I mentioned that I was coming for a show at the civic auditorium.

"Say, that's a big place," he said in disbelief.

165

"Maybe ten thousand seats. How do you expect to do?"

"Maybe we'll fill it up. They told me on the phone yesterday they had more than eight thousand sold."

"How can you do that?" he blurted out. "You're as old as I am." A rock and roll act he could believe, but not a legitimate act filling ten thousand seats. I've had this same experience a hundred times. "How can you be popular today?" they say. "You were popular when I was dating." I ask them if they still drink Coca-Cola today. And I try to explain that a performer can get better as he gets older. I know for a fact I'm a better entertainer now than at any time in my life.

My audiences now are of all ages. I especially like fairs, where whole families can watch the show in an openair atmosphere. And I put on basically the same show there as I do on the Las Vegas Strip. Recently I appeared at the Minnesota State Fair, one of my favorite locations. Just as we were about to start, a good old-fashioned Midwestern thunderstorm struck. The musicians quickly covered their instruments and rushed for cover. Lloyd Morales and a bass player and I stood there in the rain, looking out at an audience that was also waiting there patiently. I grabbed the mike and shouted, "If you ain't gonna go, neither am I!" And we kept our record intact of never missing a performance, and were as happy as kids playing tackle in the mud.

And here's another of the simple things that thrill me: I walked out into the audience one evening, and there, among the swingers and the youngsters and the celebrating couples, I saw the ever-young face of a nun—and did a double-take when I realized it was Sister Modesta, who used to bang my head against the blackboard for misspelling a word. I kissed her and told her at last, "I love you."

It thrills me to sing a song that makes a couple look longingly into each other's eyes. It thrills me to clap with people, starting out leading them, and then letting them lead me because I can't stop.

The finest compliment I ever received came years ago, but I didn't know how fine a compliment it was until I saw the effect of my Polish song. I appeared on the old "Hullabaloo" show with several of the then popular English groups. It was fashionable at that time to put down anything American. When a reporter interviewed a particular group before their return to England, he asked the expected question: What did you dislike the most about America?

Without hesitation, the lead singer said, "Mothers, apple pie, and Bobby Vinton." If he had compared me with anything or anyone else, I couldn't have been in better company. The paradox of my life in entertainment has been this: the more I showed my religion, the more tolerant I was; the more I showed my age, the closer I was in age to everyone in my audience; the more I spoke of my Polish background, the more I was an American.

NINETEEN
My Kind
of Town—
Chicago

On one of my first trips from Canonsburg to New York City, I walked up Sixth Avenue to that legendary building on Fifty-seventh Street, Carnegie Hall. The only ticket I could afford was right up near the ceiling, and I hung on for dear life as I ascended the steep stairs. One slip, I thought, and I'd be in the orchestra pit. I don't remember what was played, or who played, but it was the opening of a whole new world for a thirteen-year-old kid. That perfect hall, an acoustical jewel designed to work without microphones or opera glasses, danced in my imagination for some twenty years before I could come back a second time, this time down on the stage.

An impresario had booked me into Carnegie Hall as the Polish song swept the country. When I arrived in New York, I discovered to my chagrin that the place was far from being sold out. "Where have you been promoting the show?" I asked.

"We took ads in *The New York Times*—"

"Wait a minute. We want the *News*, maybe something on Long Island," I said with relief. A few days after the ads ran, the "Sold Out" sign went up over the box office. That was the beginning of the happiest experience of my professional life.

On the morning of December 29, 1974, I called to cancel the limousine. Instead, I walked up Sixth Avenue in the direction of Carnegie Hall, along the same route I had taken as a teen-ager. Only this time it was the Avenue of the Americas. When I entered the auditorium, everything was silent. I was the first one there. I began checking the sound system, and my father arrived. He stood in the middle of the stage, looking up at the tiers of seats above him. Then he spread his arms wide and broke into an operatic aria.

Julia and Tony Walker, my "Freedomlanders," came in early, too. This was going to a big, long day for all of us. My father was wearing the Polish colors, a white shirt with a bright red blazer. Tony thought it looked particularly sharp. "If you ever get tired of it," he said, "I'll take it." My father knew how good the Walkers had been to me in rough times. In his exuberance he took off the coat at once and made a present of it to him. This was the way the day was going to go.

Outside, it was bitterly cold; inside, it was a love feast. In the hall that had meant Chopin and Horowitz for generations of musicgoers, there was also room for a Vinton. My fans were there, but it wasn't just another opportunity for star adulation. As *The New York Times* put it the next day:

> . . . In the middle of his Polish picnic, Mr. Vinton does not neglect the basics that have made him a success: he churns out easy-going songs in the smoothest manner. He has the ability also to take old songs and update them without being revolutionary about it. It's the kind of program that has a teen-ager squealing and (as happened Sunday) a couple waltzing in the aisle to celebrate 38 years of marriage. It may be kielbasy, but Mr. Vinton prepares it with high-grade professionalism.

After the show, a reception line formed outside my dressing room, extending into the icy streets. I greeted people for two hours afterward, and at midnight I bade farewell to the hall and was the last one out. It was the greatest personal triumph I've experienced. Because my father was there, it was doubly satisfying. I can never top that evening.

My shows were now becoming "Polish picnics," and people were coming to see a person rather than a singer. In Erie, Pennsylvania, I was the guest of the heroic Polish pilot who had escaped from Russia in a MIG. I began to learn more about the Polish community in cities across the country, largely through the help of publisher Chester Grabowski and Dan Kei in Buffalo and Ted Glista in Toronto. And then I came back to Chicago, the city of three million Poles.

Alderman Roman Pucinski and his close associate, Mayor Richard J. Daley, had proclaimed January 18, 1975, "Bobby Vinton Day" in recognition of what "My Melody of Love" had done for ethnic pride in the city. The mayor made me an honorary citizen and awarded me the city's Certificate of Merit, which had never before been considered for an entertainer. The press made note of the fact that the seventy-three-year-old veteran of many a political battle was running again for office and was not ignoring my effect on his Polish constituency. At a press conference to announce the award, I got my first glimpse of the politician I had only heard about in the newspapers. We hit it off at once.

I had felt something of the same kind with John Wayne, and I feel it from time to time in my audiences. This gruff political boss, so much admired and detested, praised and made fun of, was a warm human being and a character right out of my background. He announced, "I proclaim this day 'Bobby Vinton Day' in recognition of the pride he shows for his Polish heritage." He turned to me and laughed: "What do you have to say about all this?"

I looked at Pucinski and said with a straight face, "Wait'll he finds out I'm Italian." The reporters got into the spirit of the horseplay. Someone shouted, "Sing the Polish song!"

"We'll sing it together," I answered, and I gave the grand old man some coaching in the lyrics and music of the song. It may have seemed to the press that I was being used to garner votes in the Polish community—that may have been partly true. But I

171

think the full truth came only in the summer of that year, after the election, when I was back in Chicago for a benefit of various Polish causes. This time even the press noticed there was a friendship between us that wasn't politically motivated.

On the evening I was to give my performance at the Chicago Stadium, the 20,000-seat auditorium where I would be announced as the Polish Prince, Mayor Daley had been invited to dinner with King Olaf V of Norway. He sent his regrets—to the king. Roman Pucinski, the mayor, and I ate together, and then Daley came to the show to sing along with me.

There wouldn't be another election for him, but he called a press conference the next day anyway. It was at this meeting that Jeff Lyon of the *Chicago Tribune* got a glimpse of what he called "The Cracow Kid and the Man":

> They hugged, they mugged, they were loaded with schtick. . . . "Moja droga, ja cie kocham," Mayor Daley sang a cappella, as radio reporters rushed to turn on their tape recorders. Seasoned observers have heard many astonishing sounds come out of the mayor's mouth over the years—some of them in English—but this had to be a first.

Chicago had christened me the Polish Prince, but I didn't realize that I had that title even in Poland. Visitors to this country expressed amazement when they met someone who hadn't heard of the Polish

Prince. Vinton had become almost a household name in that country behind the iron curtain. For the first time in at least a generation, observers were saying that Poland and the United States were developing special ties between them. The fact that a few words in Polish, in an English song, could bring countries closer to each other seemed incredible.

Then I was invited to an event that removed my doubts. The Polish consul general in New York, Zbigniew Dembowski, hosted a ball in my honor at the consulate. I was asked to meet the Polish dignitaries in the morning. After a few ceremonial toasts with ice-cold vodka, which left me reeling, they announced plans for a goodwill tour by me at the invitation of the Polish government. A TV special, broadcast by satellite from Poland, would cap the event. At the ball that evening, attended by hundreds of guests, I happily discussed the prospect of an Eastern European tour with my family and executives from ABC Records. We could visit Chopin's birthplace and give a concert to help restore a famous castle near Warsaw that is a symbol of Polish independence. The incredible flowering of Polish pride was going on also across the Atlantic, behind the iron curtain!

Unfortunately, time and money weren't on our side. I sent a representative to the Polish capital to check the facilities and budget of Poland's nationalized TV system. What I discovered was that, like many other small countries, Poland did not have the technical capabilities in television that would have been necessary for a first-rate show by American standards. Inevitably, my TV special would be compared with

173

those that people like John Denver and Perry Como had put on abroad. I went to the U.S. networks to see if one of them would go halfway on a special. Like the record company executives who had laughed at the thought of a Polish-American song, they laughed at the idea of a Polish TV special. I decided it would be unfair to Polish people in this country to give a show that would not be deserving of their homeland. I would insist on the best technical conditions. And I wouldn't go to Poland unless I could use the media to accomplish something more than a goodwill visit. I was at an impasse.

Someone once told me that, with all the turnovers in the three major TV networks, an executive with imagination and perception would eventually come to the fore! If you think that person exists, write to him at your favorite network and ask him if he doesn't think it would be a bold and dramatic step to bring a TV special to this country from Poland. It baffles me that, with such an obvious dearth of good programming, such a show wouldn't be a financial as well as artistic success.

I am particularly saddened by the failure of the networks to pick up on this idea because TV has been so good to me on projects with mere entertainment value. I respect all the major talk-show hosts, especially my good friends Mike Douglas, Merv Griffin, Dinah Shore and Phil Donahue. Mike was with my old record company, Epic, when he produced his hit "The Men in My Little Girl's Life." Merv's show was the place where "My Melody of Love" was introduced. Both men supported me through that "storm before the calm" when I was still looking for my niche in the entertainment field. And I did fulfill my prediction that one day I would have my own television show.

Back in my early days as an opening act for Don Rickles in Las Vegas, one of the few professionals who paid much attention to my performance was a young TV producer by the name of Chris Bearde. We kept in touch, and when I advanced to a headline show on the Strip he saw the potential for a new type of variety show on television in the spirit of my fast-paced stage act. He had connections with a Canadian group in Toronto, Arthur Weinthal and Alan Chappman, and the CBS-owned and operated stations in the United States, who were looking for a host for such a show. Several hosts were being considered.

About that time, my previous record company, Epic, had put together an album entitled "Bobby Vinton's Greatest Hits," which they were selling on late-night television with per-inquiry ads. On this basis, the station runs the ads whenever they have free time, and collects so much for every sale. It happened that my album was one of the biggest sellers on TV, so when CBS asked their stations for an opinion on a host for a new variety show my name immediately jumped out. The CBS o & o's and the Toronto group signed me to a three-year contract.

It wasn't a network show, but had to be syndicated station by station. Nevertheless, through the efforts of Sandy Frank, eventually it was bought by more than one hundred stations in all the major markets of North America. (The show was owned by Chuck Barris and Buddy Granoff.) We sailed through the first year with excellent ratings, and, although TV is no substitute for a live performance, we reached a much broader audience than I could have ever had playing in clubs all my life. Unfortunately, television executives can't stand success.

The CBS people analyzed the "Bobby Vinton Show" and decided its success was due to its production and comedy and not so much to Bobby Vinton! I was reminded of the time at Epic Records when I outsold all their other performers combined: they attributed it, not to me, but to a poor job by my competition! When I saw the results of the editing of my second year's shows, I could scarcely believe it. Bobby Vinton was limited to a few appearances and the guests were prominently featured; the format was turned upside down and a lot of the spirit was taken out. The show didn't have the same feeling of fun as it had the first year. Then the ratings started to fall off, but this convinced the executives only that my first year was a fluke! They dropped their share of the backing for the show. With my budget accordingly reduced, I decided not to try to go beyond the three-year contract. Although in Canada the show was a big hit and they wanted to renew it for the fourth year. I told Art Weinthal, the head of Canadian Network, that I wanted to quit while I was ahead. It was an exciting adventure, and it coincided with the success of "My Melody of Love" to spread that message to a wide audience.

I often wonder what would have happened if Richard Daley had been a television executive instead of a mayor. . . .

TWENTY
"Showboat"

A shrewd man has said it's harder to take success than failure, but everyone wants to try the harder first! I was ruminating about this with my agent Lee Solomon one day. He represents many of the top stars in Hollywood. It occurred to me that friendships are strained by success as much as anything else. "Lee," I speculated, "does it bother you to see all these people in your life making so much money? You devote your whole career to representing people like me. And so do Stu Welz and Dick Fox and Steve Konow. You guys make an adequate salary but that's all."

Lee thought for a minute, then answered, "We're really not living that differently, are we?"

"Well—"

"Look, we both ate the same dinner tonight, didn't we?" he began.

"Yes."

"We sleep in the same hotels."

"That's right."

"And we drive the same cars, and we wear just about the same suits. The only difference is, you can afford it and I can't!" Not only have I learned a lot about the business from great characters like Lee, but I've enjoyed life because of them. They're simply nice to be around.

I was now learning a lot more about life. From my mother, I had learned to reach for the top. Now, from my father, I was learning that what *you* get out of life is what is important to you, not what other people *think* is important. My mother and father had a successful son, and more important five grandchildren. To them that was all that mattered.

My father's ways were set, he well knew. Once he accompanied me on an appearance at Harrah's in Reno. The late Bill Harrah always treated his entertainers royally, and I took the opportunity to let my father share in some of the fruits of success. We went to dinner at an exquisite restaurant, where the tab would be picked up by the club. "Dad," I said, "it's not going to cost us anything." When we were shown to our table, I tipped the captain with a big bill. My father sat for a minute, then said, "Son, if you can do that, that's fine. But it makes me nervous to pay somebody almost a day's wages just to lead us to the table and then stand by the fire. There's a spaghetti place right across the street—all you can eat for $1.50. Look, I can go there and have my beer and that'll make me happy."

He knew that success made me happy, and he wouldn't take a minute of that from me. He could see it at the Stadium in Chicago, at Carnegie Hall, at the Polish consulate ball. When we bought our home in Southern California, the purchase price was a meaningless figure, something like the national debt, to him. He was concerned that, while I was concentrating on the creative side of my business, someone would take financial advantage of me. Typically, he would laugh and say, "Thank God you've got Dolly. She watches everything." When I was making enough money to help him establish a business of his own, he preferred to keep the job he had with Coca-Cola, driving a repair truck. At first, this was a result of his experience of the depression. "At least you'll always have a place to come back to if your records don't sell," he would say. Or, "Things aren't always going to be good." It wasn't that he lacked ambition; his ambitions were focused on me, and he experienced success through me. Fifty years before our current rage of "doing your own thing," he was doing his thing—and it made him happy. They didn't call him "Showboat" for nothing. The evidence mounted that I wasn't going to go broke, but he was cautious even after my success arrived. "What if you got a sore throat?" he said. "Thirty families are going to be out of work."

Finally he allowed some small concessions. He and my mother moved to a larger home in Canonsburg, and we picked out two of the classiest-looking cars we could find. The neighbors would ask him where he worked, and he would tell them: "Coca-Cola." They assumed he was an executive, of course.

Every morning he left home, along with the other well-dressed executives in the neighborhood, in one of his fancy automobiles. At work he changed into his coveralls and took off on his rounds in his refrigeration repair truck. One day he was parked in Pittsburgh when a neighbor spotted him. "Mr. Vinton," she said, "what are you doing with that truck—in that uniform."

"Well, I *told* you I worked for Coca-Cola," he answered.

We both knew about the uncertainties of going on the road. In his heart he was always the manager, worrying about ticket sales, planning for the next date. If the crowds had once been sparse, they could be again. Even after the unusual success of "My Melody of Love," he expected the same cycle of disappointments and surprises.

We drove to Cleveland for a one-night show, scarcely a year after my mother had to hand me a glass of wine to face a meager audience in a city not so far away. The highway was crowded. She said, "I don't know where all these people are going, but I hope they don't block the people going to your show."

"Mom," I answered, "these people are *going* to my show." The Front Row Theatre there was sold out for the entire week. I can still remember the bus loads of people coming in from Panama, a Polish section of Cleveland.

But life is funny. Ironically, as things were getting better for me on the stage and monetarily, my father was growing weaker in health. A bone cancer was eating away at him. After I left that successful performance in Cleveland, he had to stay on a few days to gather his strength. During the course of the next eleven months he was in and out of Pittsburgh's Presbyterian Hospital, under the care of their fine staff and Dr. William Cooper. I was to find out what that old saying meant: "Money can't buy everything." At this point I could buy just about anything, but the thing I wanted most couldn't be bought. In the morning of February 17, 1976, after a long, gradual deterioration of his health, death came to him as my wife, my mother, and I stood helplessly by.

TWENTY-ONE
Dreams Borne
on Butterflies

If we're lucky in this life, we get one big chance to say something to the world. I had that chance when the Polish people and I struck a chord together. I'll go on making songs; I have to. But I won't know where they'll lead or what doors they'll open.

My story here has been the story of how a song can be more than the singer. Because of the fortunate timing of "My Melody of Love," a Polish prince was born anew and a lot of people, of all races and backgrounds, benefited. I would like to close my account with a dream—that this is only the beginning.

For a pop singer, this may seem grandiose. My immediate job over the next few years will be to create albums, several of which are under contract. I will be trying to find songs that reach people, touch people, move people—according to that standard that

I learned in my youth from my father and a Polish miner named Joe Gorlack. If I succeed in that, it will be enough. But I want to do more.

When I started doing this sort of thing, the goal was to come up with a single. Now, according to the dictates of popular trends, the goal is to put together an album. And an album requires a concept. When you think of some of the highly successful albums around, that word "concept" seems overblown. It's really much simpler. I put together a polka album not too long ago with the simple idea that it would be happy music that people could play continuously at a party. Its concept: a party album. Now I'm trying to capture the flavor of my stage performance, and put that on a disc.

"Roses Are Red" was knocking 'em dead, remember?

Like it or not, I'm part of an era. I bring back fond memories for my audience, of the big bands, of the big songs, of some of my own hits. But I don't want to serve up nostalgia alone. I want to give people yesterday's memories in today's music. Music helps us remember; good music helps us to remember and enjoy.

I'm out there competing with all the good musicians and singers of the day. The record companies have a word for performers who fail to capture an audience. The word is what the barber says: "Next!"

So I've taken old memories, not old songs, and put them in modern dress, in one new album of mine. I found a man in England, Phil Coulter, who has been producing some of the most popular music on the Continent and in the British Isles. I even brought over his engineer, just to get that touch on a knob. But I still remember that "Roses Are Red" knocked 'em dead because of the lyrics, the human quotient. Whenever I came to that line, "Is that your little girl?" I could see Joe Gorlack's tear on his cheek. So what I'm really doing here is singing *about* my songs rather than singing them.

Whenever things seemed to be at a low ebb throughout history, there was always someone or some idea that came along to save us. The great human family survived because its brothers and sisters came to each other's support in time of crisis. In the broad sweep of history, every race and culture has had the chance to contribute to our mutual progress. It's such a great temptation to look to a country's recent past and ask, "What have they done?" Well, what have the Greeks done for us lately, in philosophy and art? Where are the Irish contributions in physics? We're always looking for someone's culture to decline, perhaps to make our culture seem that much better. The truth is, I think, that over the centuries the contributions of all the races to our mutual welfare are about equal.

Some of the symbols of Polish contributions to the human family are an astronomer, a patriot, a musician, and a scientist. Copernicus taught us not to be content with the safe, easy explanation. Kosciusko taught us not be to content with anything less than freedom. Chopin taught us to look to our roots for

185

inspiration. And Madame Curie taught us that a woman can be at the forefront of the modern scientific world.

Four figures from Polish history. No nation owns them. They stand as signposts to anyone who respects high aspirations and courage to pursure unpopular goals. But people of Polish ancestry can study them with greater care and love, perhaps because any son should study his father.

So we have a double reason to know more about Kosciusko in America. He was one of Washington's lieutenants in our War of Independence, that most of us know. But we may not realize that he made a second trip to the young country, during the presidency of Thomas Jefferson, to help him organize and train a standing army. In the chaotic financial situation of the young republic, he was never paid for his services. He pointed out to the President that there was an irony at our very birth. Freedom was our battle cry, but slavery was a cog in our economic machine. Kosciusko knew he couldn't change our system, but he established a principle in his will that is very seldom mentioned. Any fees owed him by the republic, his will stated, were to be used to free Jefferson's slaves. This was a good half-century before the Emancipation Proclamation.

In more recent times, a Polish scholar has planted another seed that has yet to bear fruit, but that could be the dream that man has waited for throughout recorded history. The Polish people have always been in the middle of every East-West confrontation in Europe. A man by the name of Ludovic

186

Zamenhof noted that most of the outrages and wars among men have been the result of ignorance of the language of others. What people couldn't understand, they fought. So, in the late nineteenth century, he proposed an international language, Esperanto. This concept has steadily gained adherents, until it is now estimated that more than eight million people can actually speak it.

At one time, I thought it might be possible to promote the acceptance of this language by a song. I thought that at some future Olympic Games all the participants would come with the basics of the language on their tongues. Now I feel that at least Esperanto can be a symbol of what's wrong with international relations. It can be a warning that wars of words too easily lead to wars of weapons. It can be one giant word that says to the world, "First learn to speak with each other."

Perhaps Esperanto will never be a popular hit. But they tell me history has a way of repeating itself. I hope so, for another reason. I started this story by telling you about the way "My Melody of Love" changed my life. It, too, had seven strikes against it—seven major record companies turned it down before the last one I went to gave it a chance. And, as I'm writing this, I see the same thing happening to another song of mine. Once again I'm without a record company. All of my friends at ABC, who were responsible for the success of "Melody," have gone on to other things. Times change, and so do personal tastes. The new staff at ABC didn't seem to care whether I stayed with them or not. When that happens, you know it's time for a change. So we parted company. On my own, I've cut a record, "Summerlove Sensation," which I feel has a nostalgic sentiment with a contemporary sound. Again, I've made the rounds of the industry, and again the same major record companies turned me down. And once again my old friend Al Gallico listened to it and encouraged me. We knew there had to be somebody in the industry who is alert enough to take another chance on Bobby Vinton. And we found that man. The last company we went to, Electra Records, agreed to release it. Electra's Steve Wax says it'll be a hit and may be a new direction in my life. Whatever happens, I know one thing: I'll always be in there *trying*.

Many times I've been asked, if I had to do it all over again, what would I do differently. I answer that by saying that I'd probably do everything just the way I've done it. I would make the same mistakes. As much as anything else, it's the mistakes that lead to the good things in life. For instance, when I was ready for college I first tried to enter Indiana State Teachers, near Pittsburgh, because the tuition was lower. However, I wasn't accepted in the music school. I was so heartbroken that as I drove away my mother, sensing my disappointment, said jokingly, "I hope the place burns down." As it happened, a week later the music building *did* burn down! But the point of my story is that I enrolled instead at Duquesne University, and now, all these years later, I've received an honor from them that is the finest I could ever dream of. In 1978 I was awarded an honorary doctorate in music.

If I have learned anything in my years as an entertainer, it's that people desperately want to listen and to communicate. They want their children, someday, to do a better job than their generation has in talking before shooting. They want to be more open, they want to dream, they want to love. If I have tried to say anything in my songs and as a person, it's just this. Whatever your role in life, give it everything you have, and never hesitate to ask for the greatest gift for yourself. Never hesitate to ask for love.

In one of my current songs, there's this line: "Dreams borne on butterflies, two for a penny." The Polish Prince was carried to the top on such a dream. For dreams always seem so airy, so unsubstantial, so impossible for anyone to bring to life. But if I could, so can you.